SINGLE
NOT
SEPARATE

:: HOW TO MAKE THE CHURCH A FAMILY ::

Virginia McInerney

SINGLE
NOT
SEPARATE

:: HOW TO MAKE THE CHURCH A FAMILY ::

Single, Not Separate by Virginia McInerney
Published by Charisma House
A part of Strang Communications Company
600 Rinehart Road
Lake Mary, Florida 32746
www.charismahouse.com

Cover design by Eric Powell
Interior design by David Bilby
Cover photo by Stone

Copyright © 2003 by Virginia McInerney

Library of Congress Cataloging-in-Publication Data

McInerney, Virginia, 1958-
 Single, not separate / Virginia McInerncy.
        p. cm.
 ISBN: 0-88419-929-0
 1. Church work with single people. 2 Single people—Religious
life.
 I. Title.
 BV639.S5 .M35 2003
                    2002152315

03 04 05 06 07 — 87654321
Printed in the United States of America

To Mom, Dad, Nana and Papa, for giving me life and leading me to Jesus. I will remain eternally grateful.

To my extended family, for loving me in good times and bad.
Luke 22:28

Acknowledgments

The reality of being single, *not separate* was lived out in creating this book. Special thanks to Debbie Brannan for your expertise in multiple areas, special assistance in countless ways and compassionate faith-filled words; Sue Hoeffel for your brilliance and *constant* encouragement, understanding and availability; Betsy Kubacki for wise insights and abiding support; Linda and Craig Heselton for your breadth of experience and for valuing a pioneering spirit; Dennis Stranges for birthing this book by your vision and inspiration; Rich Nathan for special encouragement and years of sound teaching; Dick Masek for graciously allowing time off; John Cook for expert counsel; Beth Hackworth for helping me walk over "broken glass"; Mark Rigsby for God-inspired creativity.

For special prayer support, thank you, Virginia Samuels, Sue Radtke, Pat Hoeffel, Judy Rigsby and Dawn Shape. For special help shaping the manuscript, thank you, Sue Hohman, Lorie Rees, Tammy Lind, Marilyn Greco, Judy Niemie, Sheryl Hedges, Brenda Burkey, Elaine Hoover, Cindy Humphrey, Mary Dietz, Mary Snider, Warren Vogel and Jennifer Parker.

Thanks to those who made sure I had food, especially Maria Seaman, Jeff and Josie Grim and Jennifer Hanson. Thanks also to those who provided special support, especially my family and the McWherters, Hochstetlers, Lebsocks, Paula Clark, Jill Anderson, Danny Meyer, Kerry Davis and everyone from my home group and the Dublin home group.

Thanks to the staff of Strang Communications, especially Lee Grady, Dave Welday, Barbara Dycus, Ann Mulchan and Maureen Haner.

For life-changing input, thank you, Lois Myer, Joyce Meyer and Bob and Kathy Muni.

Contents

Introduction

You might be surprised to find yourself reading a "singles book." If that's the case, trust me, I understand. There was a time I would have been surprised to find myself reading a singles book, because I didn't (and still don't) want to be single. The only singles book I would have been interested in reading was one that helped me NOT BE SINGLE any longer! But then, also to my surprise, I've remained single for far longer than I ever expected or wanted.

As the years progressed, I found myself increasingly challenged by my singleness and increasingly in need of answers to the tough things I was facing. Unfortunately, resources to help me were few and far between. Sure, there were books on dating and books that centered on contentment as a single, but I couldn't find much that addressed many of my day-to-day struggles. I also couldn't find any that simply validated what I was feeling and experiencing. I began wondering if I were the only one feeling these things. *Is it just me?* I thought. *Am I crazy?*

Over time the Lord has opened my eyes to many singles who have experienced and felt the same things I have—things written about in the pages you hold in your hands. It's not just me! And it's not just you.

As I came to realize this, I was comforted to know I wasn't alone, and I wasn't crazy. I was grateful for the comfort, but I wanted more than comfort—I wanted answers and solutions. Sure, I'd rather be married, period. But for the time that I remained single, I wanted to know ways to make my life better.

The more I sought God, the more He gave me answers. Then He called me to begin making these solutions more widely known. Two things now fuel me:

1. I honestly believe the concepts in this book work. I've experienced them working for me and witnessed them working for others.

2. I truly believe that if I had known these things years ago, I'd have been better off in every way over these last two decades. I want to spare others from needless searching and suffering.

The content is laid out in two parts. The first part takes a head-on approach to many of the questions we find rolling around in our heads. These identify frustrations we face, some of which are generated by misperceptions held about singles. People who were not single for long generally don't have an experience base from which to understand our perspective. So some of the things we grapple with arise from that lack of understanding. The better you understand these issues, the better equipped you'll be to successfully address these areas in your own life. Not only that, but you'll be better able to help others understand these issues, which ultimately is good for us all.

We're going to get to the "how to make the church a family" part, but first we're going to take care of you. Because that's what families do. And in order for you to be contributing to the family as you'd like, first you have to be doing OK yourself. It's hard to be doing OK when all the issues discussed in Part I are swirling around in your head and heart and beating you down.

The second part of the book casts vision for changes I believe God is bringing about within the church—changes that will make us more like the family God intended us to be. It is good for us to want others in our lives whom we love and who love us. But I have found it difficult, as a single, to sustain the level of relationship I believe God wants me to have. Various barriers inhibit this, and He wants to remove them. He wants to open the floodgates to abundantly meet the relational needs of singles today!

And there are lots of us! Did you know that 46 percent of American adults are single? That's what the 2000 United States census told us.[1] Even if we extract out the younger singles, 36 percent of the population over twenty-four years old is single.[2] Does that surprise you? When you think about your church, does it *seem* like nearly half the congregation is not married? More than likely your answer is *no*—whether or not your church mirrors the national norm—because your church probably looks and feels like a "couples church." We need to adjust this unintentional imbalance to better reflect who we truly are as God's family.

The best way to attain more balance is to break down the wall of division between couples and singles. Bridging this gap is one of the most important things we can do to make the church a family. So we take a close look at that. We also look at how we fit into a newly blended and integrated church. By the time you reach the end of this book, you'll have examined and resolved personal issues of your own, considered revisions to make in your closest relationships, and learned how to become change agents in the larger domain of your church.

I'm going to equip you with information and perspective that will enhance your own life, believing you'll also want to be used by God to spread this helpful information to others. While it's wonderful to improve your own life, it's joy beyond measure to improve the lives of others. My earnest hope is that as you understand the things written herein, you'll want to communicate what you've learned to others. You can't make the church a family all by yourself. We all need to be involved in that process. If that's going to happen, you'll need to help others around you understand the things written in this book. So read it for all it's worth. Throw your whole heart into it. If you do, and if others do, in due season, we'll see God transform His church into a family that understands, loves and embraces singles and couples alike. Catch the vision. Then, run with the vision. Run hard and far and wide.

Chapter 1

Perspectives

Before we dive into things, I want to clarify my perspective on a few key points. First, when I say "singles" I am referring to adults who are not married, whether they have never been married, are divorced or are widowed—no matter their age. I do, however, need to make an important distinction involving age.

Much of what I describe in this book generally is not descriptive of singles under age twenty-five. Singles under this age don't *feel* the label "single" yet. It's likely that they simply think of themselves as adults in the normal progression of their lives who just haven't married yet. Many of the things I describe don't reflect how younger singles feel because they have not reached the age where being single becomes an issue or a concern.

There is great diversity among singles—never married, divorced with no children, single parents, widowed, younger, middle-aged and older. Given the wide variations among us, it is not possible to make generalities that describe all singles at all times. I have not modified every statement to apply to each category of singles. I trust you will simply set aside the generalizations that don't apply to you.

On points that are not uniformly applicable to all categories of singles, the perspective in this book tends to align more with the experience of never-married singles. They comprise the largest percentage of the total single population (61 percent).[1] The unique needs arising from divorce or the loss of a spouse, especially when children are involved, deserve more attention than what is possible here.

WHO ARE TODAY'S SINGLES?[2]

Age	Separated	Divorced	Widowed	Never Married
15–24	.005	.003%	0%	99%
25–29	5%	9%	0%	85%
30–34	7%	22%	1%	69%
35–44	10%	40%	3%	47%
45–54	8%	52%	8%	31%
55–64	7%	49%	26%	18%
Over 64	3%	15%	73%	9%
Total singles	5%	20%	14%	61%

I approach this subject believing the majority of us would prefer to marry if we find the right person. I've read books and articles stating that it is a *myth* that most singles want to get married. I disagree. Statistics tell us otherwise. According to the 2000 U.S. Census, by age fifty-five, only 4.9 percent of American adults were never married. By age sixty-five, this percentage drops to 3.6 percent.[3] Also, 93 percent of Americans rank having a happy marriage as an important life objective.[4] Of people who divorce, 75 percent remarry.[5]

These are convincing indicators that most of us would prefer to marry! Sure, some will prefer to remain single for a season of life. But I highly doubt many people would answer *yes* if asked "Do you wish to remain single the rest of your life?"

The main objective in this book is not to tell you, "Just be content and make the best of it." Quite likely you've heard that enough already! Being and staying content, and knowing how to maintain desires that are healthy, yet unfulfilled, are difficult and complicated. I don't oversimplify that issue.

I also don't intend to talk you into *loving* the single life. I'm aiming at a different objective for different reasons. I'm going to point out the reasons why living single is harder than it needs to be due to the culture—especially our "Christian culture." However, in striving toward that goal, I don't want this book to become a tool for people to commiserate with one another! I don't hold a "victim" mentality, and I certainly don't want to encourage you to either.

I strongly believe that God wants to validate many of the things you have felt. I will illustrate some of those experiences, but not so that we can say, "Oh, poor me!" My ultimate purpose is to give pertinent examples that provide fresh perspectives. Prayerfully, God will use those perspectives to usher in change. If you'll run with the vision set forth in these pages, I believe your life will be a lot easier to love—regardless how long you remain single.

Part I

Questions Singles Ask

Part I is written in a question-and-answer format to make it easy for you to find some quick, basic answers to problematic issues. The responses are by no means exhaustive. An entire book could be written to address these questions adequately. I've written "bullet" answers—responses that touch on the high points of the issues raised. I've also incorporated both practical and theoretical answers. Getting these questions out in the public domain puts them on the table for further discussion by others who also have learned a great deal through experience. The more we pass around the tools God has given us, the better it is for everyone.

Here's a caution before you start reading. After looking at any *one* of these responses, it would be easy to say, "Oh, well, fine, but that's not going to *really* help me." I realize that. Applying a few of the answers to the issues you face may feel like only a drop in the bucket. But if you'll apply as many as you can, cumulatively, these *will* make a difference. Avoid the temptation to write off a suggestion as *too insignificant*. It's the overall effect that counts.

Change won't come immediately. You have to be patient. We sow seeds, but often, the harvest comes much later. Press on even when you don't see immediate relief or improvement. Don't quit! Diligently apply yourself. Many of the responses must be learned and practiced. There is a learning curve with every skill. Often we are tempted to quit somewhere along the line—usually right before we finally master a skill. Stay at it!

> Let us not lose heart in doing good, for in due time we shall reap if we do not grow weary.
> —GALATIANS 6:9

Chapter 2

Theological Issues

Q **What do I do if I am angry with God because He has not given me a spouse?**

A Some of us get angry with God, even though we know this is sin. Rationally, we know that it makes no sense to be angry with God. After all, the Bible says that He is good and loving and kind and every other conceivable perfect characteristic. Those characteristics are in our *minds* regarding our knowledge of God. But there is the proverbial "twelve-inch drop" between our head and our heart. That's where the problem lies.

One reason it is so hard to win this battle over anger directed at God is because everywhere we turn there are reminders of what we *want* but *don't have*. These incessant reminders continually fuel our longings and desires, day after day, season after season, year after year. As we head into another Christmas season, we think, *I'm alone again this Christmas. How many more Christmases must I endure this? Will it ever end?* Each season carries a reminder that time is passing, and you are still alone.

It is the *constancy* of facing frustrated longings that fuels the temptation to be angry with God. Anger about your situation builds inside, and you want to blame somebody. It seems like it is *God's fault*. In His sovereignty, this is what He's chosen, or allowed, for you, and you disdain it. So He becomes the object of your anger. Thus a spiritual dilemma rears its ugly head. What do you do with this stick of dynamite? In holy fear, you tremble at the thought of being angry with Him, but you are stuck.

The good news is that God is merciful, patient, compassionate and understanding. He beckons you to get your pain out in the open, even though you have no "right" to be angry with Him. He knows what is in your heart anyway, so hiding it is futile.

The Lord began to deal with me about the anger toward Him stewing inside me. I knew I had to admit it, but I was afraid to do so. My head told me, *You can't express that to God…I mean, this is God we're talking about. The Creator of the universe—the One who made you and all you see. You can't yell at God.*

One day several things went wrong in rapid succession, and I blew up. As I drove to a church seminar, of all things, I started to yell at God. Interspersed with my yelling were all kinds of apologies, such as, "I'm sorry I feel this way. I know You are God, and I'm afraid to be telling You this. You have every right to strike me with a bolt of lightning. But this is how I feel." The Bible says that God desires truth in the innermost being (Ps. 51:6). I was telling God the truth about how I felt and what I thought. My thoughts were wrong. My feelings were the direct result of my wrong thinking, but it all had to come up and out.

God was the only One who could help me out of that dark place. By stuffing it down inside, I had been turning my back on Him in hostility and fear. The starting place out was to be honest. At least then I was *connecting* with God. I had opened an entry point for God to straighten out my thinking.

I'm not condoning being angry with God. It's sin. But we can't just pretend it isn't there. We can't make it go away by a sheer act of our will. Acknowledging it by being honest is the starting point. Confession follows. Then God forgives us and cleanses us (1 John 1:9).

Things really began to change for me after that. In a very personal and tangible way, I experienced God's kindness to me as He permitted me to vent. I knew He had every right, as a *holy God*, to put me in my place. But instead He took upon

Himself all my rage. He put the sin I was spewing out on Jesus instead of turning on me with righteous wrath. This is what it means in Romans 2:4 when Paul states that "the kindness of God leads you to repentance."

In this way, God softened my heart and caused me to see His true character again. I had fallen prey to the deceptive thinking that God was cruel because He was putting me through, or allowing me to go through, so much pain.

Moses, Job and David all became angry with God. I believe God recorded their angry outbursts to illustrate that we may encounter things in life that provoke us to be angry with God. Great people of faith have experienced anger toward God. He understands our humanity, and He is merciful.

Q **Why does God allow us to go through the pain of singleness?**

A Theologians and philosophers have wrestled for centuries with the problem of suffering. It seems contradictory—a contradiction summed up well in this statement by C. S. Lewis:

> If God were good, He would wish to make His creatures perfectly happy, and if God were almighty, He would be able to do what He wished. But the creatures are not happy. Therefore, God lacks either goodness or power or both.[1]

We know that God does not lack these attributes, so we find ourselves perplexed over the subject of pain. For us, it isn't merely theoretical—it's very personal. We are plagued with questions regarding God's purpose and allowance of suffering; they're right at our doorstep, right in our own hearts. We know that God could easily give us a spouse, but He hasn't. Some of us wrestle with the issue that He did not provide a spouse in time for us to have children.

The Bible does not give any quick, easy, *apparent* answers to this issue. The Bible does not come right out and say, "The reason suffering exists in the world is because..." It does, however, address the issue—but it does so primarily by repeatedly demonstrating four main truths:

- God gives us freedom, and we choose to sin.
- God works through suffering.
- God more than compensates for our suffering.
- God is with us in our suffering—even though we may feel He isn't.[2]

The more thoroughly acquainted we are with these truths, the better we can apply them to our circumstances and overcome temptations to "fault" God or question His goodness for allowing us to experience the pains associated with being single.

The main issue regarding the problem of suffering is God's character. When we suffer, we are tempted to say that God is not good. But God is good even though we cannot definitively answer the question *Why?* regarding suffering. Ultimately, when we consider that God not only suffers *with us*, but, most importantly, He suffered *for us*, we find resolution. Our sin separated us from God because He is holy and we are not. In order to bring us into a personal relationship with Himself, God paid the ultimate price for our sin, which is death. He died in our place. The Bible says the sins of the whole world were laid upon Him. Out of love, God freely chose to take upon Himself the just penalty for our sin. He suffered on our behalf more than any human being ever has or ever will suffer.

In fact, He Himself experienced *all* the suffering that has ever resulted from sin. Thus we can know for certain that God understands everything we feel and is feeling it right along with us. Does He *care* that it hurts? Yes, He does, very much. When you are tempted to disbelieve God's goodness, remember that He brings good out of bad and compensates for our pain. Most importantly, He showed us that He Himself was willing to endure the worst pain possible in sacrifice for us so that ultimately, one day, we would no longer experience pain.[3]

Q **How do I deal with haunting, sometimes unanswerable questions like these: "Is there something wrong with me?" "Is the reason I am not married because of past mistakes?"**

A All of us, married and single, have questions that may not be answered on this side of heaven. Still, Jesus welcomes us to ask. Many times He does answer our specific and direct questions. Sometimes He does not, for reasons we don't know. But in either case, it all comes down to faith.

If we do get a sense about God's answer to a question we pose, it takes faith to believe that the answer truly is from God. We know that it may be just our own thoughts, or we may be wrongly interpreting a set of circumstances. At some point, we have to take a step of faith in what we believe. In principle, this is similar to our first confession of faith in Jesus Christ as our Savior. We had no *absolute* proof, but God graced us with the faith to believe. We continue our walk through life in the same way. "As you therefore have received Christ Jesus the Lord, so walk in Him" (Col. 2:6).

If we don't get an answer to a question, we must again exercise our faith. We need to believe that:

- God has His reasons for not answering.

- He is good even if His lack of response *to us* makes it seem as if He is not good.

- What the Bible says about God, and about us, is true even when our experience seems to contradict that.

- If God truly does want us to know the answer to the question, He will tell us at a later time.

Believing what is true about God's character and nature ultimately resolves our questions, even if we don't get answers. We know that God loves us. Consequently, we can rest in knowing that He does have a good plan for our lives. Romans 8:28 says that He works all things together for good for those who love Him and are called according to His purpose. This means that even without knowing the answer to our questions, we can rest in knowing that God can make everything turn out all right in the end. Even if the reason you currently are not married happens to be because of past mistakes, God can use those mistakes and redeem them, turning them into something that is good.

As for the question, "Is the reason because there's something wrong with me?"—well, ultimately the answer to that question need not matter. There's something wrong with everyone, married or single. "For all have sinned..." (Rom. 3:23). If there is something about you that actually is a hindrance to marriage, God can take care of it, no matter what it is. Ask Him to address any issue that may be standing in the way. Then yield to Him when He does. Focus your attention on God's ability to resolve problems more than on the question itself.

Q **Is the reason I'm not married yet because I am not "refined" enough?**

A It is fairly *common* for singles to hear well-meaning Christian friends and family use this concept. If a person doesn't use the word *refined*, something like it is used in its place. The concept is that you'd be married but for the fact that God still has some work He wants to do in your character—conforming you more into His image before He's going to give you a mate. People liken the word *refined* in Scripture, indicating God's process of sanctifying us, to the refining of silver. (See Psalm 66:10; Isaiah 48:10; Zechariah 13:9.)

All of us are in the process of being refined. "He who began a good work in you will perfect it until the day of Christ Jesus" (Phil. 1:6). But that's just it—we all are being refined. It is a lifelong process. God may have certain things He wants to do in your life before He brings you a spouse.

But although all of us are being refined, we cannot say *universally* that needed refinement in a person is *the reason* why *every* person who hasn't married yet is not married. That is far too simplistic. If someone kindly offers this to you as the reason you are not yet married, remember that we *all* are being refined continuously, and that may have *nothing* to do with the reason God hasn't given you a spouse. Whatever you do, don't internalize this and continuously speculate about all kinds of faults in yourself that need improving. You may become depressed if you focus too much on your faults. That is not good for anyone. Instead, look to God, and trust Him to do His good work in you—trusting Him also to give you a spouse at the right time.

What do I do when I feel as if God has abandoned or, worse, betrayed me?

God is the only One who can give us the desires of our heart, and we must resist taking matters into our own hands. We know He easily could grant our desires, so when He doesn't, it provokes *Why?* questions. "Why me?" "Why must I wait so long?" "Why have You blessed most of my friends but not me?" "Why did You allow me to marry a person You knew would be unfaithful?" "Why couldn't I have children?"

When we ask these types of questions, we're seeking to understand something important about *God*—His nature and character. In the questions we asked earlier we were seeking to

understand something imperative about *ourselves*. This distinction makes a huge difference in the way we view God's response
to these questions.

These *Why?* questions arise out of very significant issues
that potentially shape much of our adult lives. Therefore,
these questions are weighty. It is not the same as asking, "God,
why did You allow me to break my leg?" or "Why was my
vacation such a disaster?" As you continue life as a single,
these questions may get heavier and heavier as you agonize to
find answers and try to make sense of it all when God seems
silent. Your head can tell you that He has not left you, for He
has promised, "I will never desert you, nor will I ever forsake
you" (Heb. 13:5). However, your heart aches over your confusing reality. Once again you face the spiritual dilemma of
the "twelve-inch drop" between your head and your heart.

The next step down from abandonment is betrayal. We
know that God is omnipotent, so He can intervene in every
situation. When He does not respond in the way that seems
loving or needed, you are tempted to believe that God has
betrayed you. Perhaps you pray for years, with increasing
intensity, to marry, but remain single. Maybe all your friends
and family keep praying for you, and still God seems unre-
sponsive. Over time, it becomes harder to resist believing that
God has betrayed you.

You know that God could not betray you, for He gave His
very life for you (John 3:16). But in your pain and confusion,
you can begin caving in to the lie that He does not care or, at
best, is indifferent. If you yield to that lie, you will grow bitter and resentful and may even turn your back on God.

The next struggle that we may experience is facing squarely
the issue of God's sovereignty. While these plaguing, unre-
solved dilemmas can lead in many directions, ultimately either
you will accept God's sovereignty or turn your back on it. You
must come face to face with the stark reality of whether or not
you can truly say, "Though he slay me, yet will I trust in him"

(Job 13:15, KJV). Unless you arrive at that attitude of heart, you will remain stuck somewhere in limbo between accepting and denying God's sovereignty.

The easiest thing to do is to try to ignore that issue altogether. But ignoring it makes you incapable of moving ahead with God into all the fullness He intends for you. Consequently, you will hit a plateau and stay there. How tragic.

I don't condone these responses, but I do understand them because I have faced them. Much of my earlier energy was spent resisting the temptations that accompany these dilemmas. There were very black times when I caved in—worse than feeling that you've lost your best friend. You feel as if you've lost your compass. You don't know how to find your way out of that dark place. This can happen to the most sincere, earnest, fervent Christians. In Isaiah 50:10 we read:

> Who is among you that *fears* the LORD,
> That *obeys* the voice of His servant,
> That walks in darkness and has no light?
> Let him *trust* in the name of the LORD and *rely* on his
>   God.
>
>   —EMPHASIS ADDED

In this place, Jesus truly is your *Savior*, for you cannot save yourself. All you can do is trust Him to rescue you. And He does.

Often He does so through His people. First Thessalonians 5:14 tells us to "encourage the fainthearted, help the weak, be patient with all men." We can and should help others who are in this dreadful, dark place to become strong in faith once again. Anyone who has fallen prey to any of these temptations knows how awful it is to feel separated from the only One who can help you. Sometimes you need to see His face through the face of a person whom He can use to reconnect you with your Best Friend.

When you have exhausted all your energy and will by struggling to understand the answers to questions that are

beyond you, it really is OK to give up that fight. It is not a sign
of weakness to lower your head and say, "God, I just don't
understand." Neither are you a "bad" Christian for vigorously
asking these hard questions and seeking answers in the first
place. God does not despise you for asking, and you should
not despise yourself for quitting the quest, as long as you end
your quest in trust, not defeat. The greatest peace comes not
in understanding the answers to our plaguing questions but in
a submitted heart that rests in the knowledge of God's goodness despite everything that may argue to the contrary. God
will get you to this place if you let Him.

Q **Is God all I need? When I open up and admit
my longings for relationship, people respond
by advising me to deepen my relationship with
Jesus. Why do I still yearn for something more?**

A The false notion that singles are to derive *all* their
relational satisfaction solely from their relationship
with Jesus has made the lives of singles more challenging than need be. This is such an ingrained concept that
you're probably thinking, *Well, isn't that true?*

While it certainly is true that Jesus is the *ultimate* source
through which all our needs, relational and otherwise, are
met, He meets those needs in diverse ways. Sometimes He
does so directly, but often He does so indirectly through
people, circumstances or something else.

I suspect that most Christian singles, when voicing relational needs, have been admonished to develop a deeper relationship with God. My guess is that they were given that
advice in a manner implying that relationships with people are
not truly necessary. They may even have been told, "You just
need to focus on your relationship with God. Go deeper with
Jesus. He will satisfy you."

While there is truth to these statements that applies to us *all*,
married and single, there also is a distortion that winds up

hurting singles. Think about this. You bring up a relational need. You are then redirected to Jesus for fulfillment. Because you bring this up in the context of *human* relationships, you can easily interpret this type of response as saying, "It is wrong to look for relational satisfaction through people; look for it only in God Himself. He is enough." You can easily come under false guilt upon hearing such statements. What kind of response can you give to that? You can't say, "No, God is not enough." Your mouth is shut when receiving this kind of counsel. It becomes a bondage from which you must know how to break free!

Let's sort out this twisted truth. Many scriptures point to the *necessity* of human companionship. In addition to principles we glean from Genesis 2:18, which we'll discuss in Part II, here are some additional key scriptures about companionship:

> Two are better than one because they have a good return for their labor. For if either of them falls, the one will lift up his companion. But woe to the one who falls when there is not another to lift him up. Furthermore, if two lie down together they keep warm, but how can one be warm alone? And if one can overpower him who is alone, two can resist him. A cord of three strands is not quickly torn apart.
> —ECCLESIASTES 4:9–12

> The Lord appointed seventy-two others and sent them two by two ahead of him…
> —LUKE 10:1, NIV

In addition to these verses, in Exodus 17:10–12, we see that even the spiritual giant Moses—who was the "friend of God," one who knew God face to face—needed Aaron and Hur to hold up his arms while he interceded for Israel during battle.

In the Epistles alone there are over fifty references to "one another"—"Love one another;" "Forgive one another;" "Serve one another." God places great value on our relationships. We were not meant to live life with God alone. We are made in His image—an image that deeply desires relationship. While our relationship with God is *primary*, we need each other, too.

A single woman contacted me expressing sincere concern about her desire for relationships. She had been listening to the words of a popular Christian song that repeated lyrics about God being all we need. In addition, she had received some counsel that provoked her to wonder whether it was wrong for her to desire relationships with others. She wanted to please God and was quite troubled that she might be displeasing Him. She asked whether she needed to relinquish completely all her desires for human relationships.

I have seen singles fall into this same quagmire over and over again. For a deeper look at this issue, see *12 Christian Beliefs That Can Drive You Crazy: Relief from False Assumptions* by Dr. Henry Cloud and Dr. John Townsend. Read "Assumption 7—If I Have God, I Don't Need People."[4]

The problem with this twisted truth goes further than just leaving us feeling guilty about our desires for human relationship. Here's what can happen. Let's say "John" receives an admonition to obtain total relational satisfaction in Jesus. In sincerity, he earnestly tries. But because God designed us differently, he fails. Then he begins to wonder what is wrong with him. He wonders why he can't get close enough to God to satisfy his unmet relational needs. What more must he do? Now he is left with a false belief that his relationship with God is flawed in some way. This type of struggle only exacerbates the relational strain singles endure. It can push some people over the edge into feeling like a failure when it comes to human relationships (presumed because they are not yet married). They may also feel like a failure in their relationship with their heavenly Father. We need to work hard to set singles free from this horrible cycle.

Hopefully you now see that desires for human relationships are normal and healthy. God does not look upon you with disfavor for having such desires. If you've been walking under a cloud of guilt over this, be free!

Q **What do I make of the teaching that it is "better" to be single?**

A First Corinthians 7 is the chapter people cite in asserting that it is better to be single than married. The verses at issue are verses 7–9 and 25–40. I'll highlight some key portions:

> But I say to the unmarried and to widows that it is good for them if they remain even as I…Now concerning virgins I have no command of the Lord, but I give an opinion as one who by the mercy of the Lord is trustworthy. I think then that this is good in view of the present distress, that it is good for a man to remain as he is…One who is unmarried is concerned about the things of the Lord, how he may please the Lord; but one who is married is concerned about the things of the world, how he may please his wife, and his interests are divided…This I say…to secure undistracted devotion to the Lord…So then both he who gives his own virgin daughter in marriage does well, and he who does not give her in marriage will do better…In my opinion she [a widow] is happier if she remains as she is.
>
> —1 Corinthians 7:8, 25–26, 32–35, 38, 40

A common thread runs through the commentaries I've read on these verses. Bible scholars seem to agree that one of Paul's primary objectives was to exhort all Christians, both married and single, to focus on the things of God more than on things of this world, which are passing away. (See 1 John 2:15–17; Matthew 6:19–21.) In addition, nearly all the commentaries I read said Paul's advice to remain single came in an era of great persecution to the church, when remaining single would lessen the heartache suffered and the disruption to family life caused when married persons were tortured or martyred. It was easier for singles to uproot abruptly to flee persecution. Some commentaries also interpreted these verses to affirm singleness as a legitimate lifestyle because Paul was writing during a time of arranged marriages and when being single was a reproach.

The principles Paul states in these verses are timeless, although the portion of his message that applies to living in a time of persecution does not apply to American singles today. It does, however, apply to Christian brothers and sisters in other parts of the globe where Christians are being persecuted. One important aspect of Paul's message does apply to American singles—that *all of us, married and single, should be devoted to God first and foremost.*

> But seek first His kingdom and His righteousness; and all these things shall be added to you.
>
> —MATTHEW 6:33

Jesus was asked this question: "Teacher, which is the great commandment in the Law?" (Matt. 22:36).

We clearly see Jesus' desire that we be devoted first and foremost to God in the answer He gave: "You shall love the Lord your God with all your heart, and with all your soul, and with all your mind. This is the great and foremost commandment" (vv. 37–38).

It seems that the main distinction Paul was making between singles and couples in 1 Corinthians was that singles could be more devoted to God because they were not as distracted as couples. Why does this seem to be so far from reality for us now? I don't feel less distracted by worldly matters than couples, and as I look around, it seems this is true of most singles I know. By this, I don't mean that singles are less *devoted*; I just don't see a big difference between couples and singles with respect to the potential for distraction. So why were the singles of Paul's day less distracted?

It has to come down to the cultural differences between Paul's day and ours. Bible scholars hold that Scripture must be interpreted in light of the culture in which it was written. Some texts describe truth purely through the words, while others, to be properly understood, must be viewed through a cultural glass and then applied properly to today's culture.[5]

The culture of gospel times was obviously very different from ours. Singles then had a very different experience than in today's highly individualistic America. They continued living in the context of family. (See 1 Corinthians 7:37, and consider Mary, Martha and Lazarus's living arrangements.) Families lived in a strong community environment. Additionally, singles, as a general rule, did not remain single late into life. So singles back in Paul's day were not so "out there" as we are today, when, for example, 26 percent of us live alone. I believe they were freer to have undivided interests because many of their basic needs, especially for companionship, were being met in that cultural environment. Many of their responsibilities were shared with others. If many of my needs were being taken care of in a more corporate sense, as were the needs of singles of Paul's day, then yes, I do believe I could devote more time directly to my relationship with Jesus and in service to others.

But as it is now, much of my time, of necessity, must be devoted to being responsible for myself. Thus, my life today is rife with opportunity for "distractions." I am distracted by trying to maintain the level of companionship I legitimately need to remain emotionally healthy. I am distracted by being *solely* responsible for every aspect of my life. I cannot shirk these responsibilities. God expects me to act responsibly so that I don't force others to take care of my duties. So it is appropriate that I "concern" myself with these matters. This reality is exponentially multiplied for single parents.

If it truly was better to be single in today's culture, I feel certain we'd see evidence of that. Our experience does not dictate truth, but it can underline God's principles. So first, I ask, how many people do you know who feel genuinely that being single is better than being married and, if given a choice, would prefer to remain single? Even those in bad marriages often don't want to be single. They just want to be in a *good* marriage. This is evidenced by the fact that even after experiencing a hard marriage, most divorcees (75 percent) prefer to remarry.[6]

Second, how many books extol the virtues of being single? Are they easily believable, or do they seem to be trying hard to convince you that it can be true? Treatment of the subject runs more along the lines of teaching singles how to live single as effectively as possible, rather than holding it up as a *preferable* lifestyle. Third, if it was such a preferable lifestyle, why would 94 percent of our Protestant pastors be married, not single?[7] If doubt remains, simply read *The Case for Marriage: Why Married People Are Happier, Healthier, and Better Off Financially* by Linda J. Waite and Maggie Gallagher.[8] The authors raise compelling arguments making it quite difficult to assert that it is, in fact, better to be single in today's culture.

Incidentally, over the years, I've made it a practice to ask my single friends, after they marry, if they prefer marriage over being single. No one has told me they thought being single was better—and I'm talking about mature people who were earnestly seeking and serving God as singles and continue to do so as married persons.

It is important to interpret correctly this passage, because improper interpretation has negatively impacted singles. Proper interpretation releases us from guilt we may have carried for desiring marriage. It frees us to want to be married. It legitimizes many of the things we may have felt but were reluctant to admit regarding our belief that being single was not necessarily better. For those who truly are called to remain single, it is better to be single. But for those who are not called, we need to acknowledge the legitimacy of their view that singleness is not preferable to marriage.

Let's not spend our time and energy trying to convince ourselves that our lifestyle is supposed to be preferable to marriage. Instead, we should encourage one another to spend time building a more supportive culture for both singles and couples so that we all can follow as hard after God as possible. Consider how powerful singles could be if undergirded by a strong sense of community!

Q **Does the simple fact that I *am* single mean I have been "called" to be single (for life)?**

A I doubt people honestly believe that God has specifically *called* nearly half of the population in America to be single. Unfortunately, some people do assume that if you are single, particularly an older, never married single, God has called you to be single for life. Some are called to a lifetime of singleness, but many are single for some other reason.

Let's look at this presumption of a call to singleness. Just because something exists in this world, do we automatically believe God has specifically decreed that it be? We know that He is omnipotent and sovereign. But does everything that happens in this world happen as He *wanted* (not willed) it to? No. For example, He does not *want* people to sin (even though He works even that for His plan and purposes). Here's another example. By the mere existence of cancer, do we assume that God "calls" people to have cancer? Does He "call" people to wheelchairs? Does He "call" for war? We know that He can heal a person's cancer and raise one from a wheelchair. We know that He is deeply moved by the enormous and untold pain suffered by those who know war firsthand. What we don't know is why some painful things in life are allowed to continue, while others are resolved.

Truly, some are called to be single. God gives them the

grace to walk in that calling. But I believe there is quite a difference between the one who is *called* and the one who simply remains single.

To better understand this, it is helpful to draw an analogy to couples who are unable to conceive. Do we automatically say that God has "called" them to remain barren? We pray for them and then leave the results in God's hands. We never really quite know, as we pray, why they are barren. Is it because…

- God, in fact, is specifically *calling* them to be childless?

- Satan is robbing them (John 10:10)?

- It is simply not God's time (Gal. 4:4; 6:9)?

- There is an issue they must deal with personally before God will bestow the blessing (Acts 3:19; James 5:16; 1 Pet. 3:7; 1 John 1:9)?

The same principle applies with respect to the issue of singleness. Some of us are called, some are robbed, some must wait longer, some must resolve personal issues. But we don't know which it is for which person. So people should not oversimplify this and say that just because a person *is* single, it must mean that God has *called* him or her to be single and remain single.

It seems safe to assume that God has not called nearly half the population to be single for two additional reasons. First, the Bible seems to imply that those who truly are called to a lifetime of singleness are few. Second, the vast majority of people do in fact marry at some point in their lives.

A proper understanding of this issue can produce something very sweet in the body of Christ. I believe this understanding will engender a greater degree of compassion for those who are single against their will—those who do not sense God has *called* them to be single. Much like the couple who yearns to hold a baby, many of us yearn for a mate. The pain is real, and for many, it is not God's calling that is producing this pain.

There is a balance to strike. God may call you to be single for a *season*. It's difficult for us to embrace this because of the teaching hanging over our heads that seems to make it an all-or-nothing proposition. That is, either you are called to be single, or you are called to be married. We need to balance this concept by helping others see how common it is that a person be called to singleness for a *season*, but not necessarily for life. Assuming that after a certain age a person has been called to be single (for life) makes embracing being single (for a season) that much harder. Instead of readily yielding and even enjoying a season of being single, this assumption leaves you struggling with a lifetime of something to which God may not actually have called you. If He hasn't called you, He hasn't graced you for that.

I believe this view of singleness has an incredibly strong hold on singles today, and it is choking the life that could be lived. It is harder to "look on the bright side" of being single when you project your current reality into the future for life and cannot imagine living the rest of your life that way. As we age, many of us find it harder to believe we will marry, in large part because of this mind-set. Before age thirty, many may encourage you, saying, "God will provide a mate for you." But as the years roll on, fewer people make those statements, and fewer pray along these lines for you. Rather than staking our beliefs based on the *perceived* societal norms, we need to stake our beliefs on God's plan for a person. As Rich Nathan, the senior pastor of Vineyard Church of Columbus, has said, "God's delays are not always His denials." When viewed from this perspective, we can *genuinely* encourage each other that God will provide a spouse if and when He sees fit, and that just may be when you are forty-five instead of twenty-five. In the meantime, God will use a period of singleness to conform you into His image.

Chapter 3

Dealing With Emotions

Q **How do I get past feeling that it is impossible to be happy and enjoy life while single?**

A The root of this problem is our difficulty believing that God approves of our happiness. Before going further with this answer, first read the following scriptures:

DOES GOD WANT ME TO BE HAPPY?

Deuteronomy 16:15	Psalm 90:14
Psalm 4:7	Psalm 92:4
Psalm 5:11	Psalm 97:11
Psalm 16:11	Ecclesiastes 3:1–13
Psalm 21:6	Isaiah 35:10
Psalm 23:6	Isaiah 51:3, 11
Psalm 27:13–14	Isaiah 65:18
Psalm 30:11	Lamentations 3:21–25
Psalm 32:11	Habakkuk 3:17–19
Psalm 68:3	

For me, the crux of this issue rested in answering, "What do I believe about God's nature and what He wants for me?" Does He want me to be happy? Does my happiness even matter to God? Or are there other more important things on His agenda like character building and kingdom building? Does my being happy *always* take a back seat to other more important and noble goals?

At some point along my Christian walk, I picked up the notion that seeking to be happy was almost tantamount to sin.

Joy was OK, but happiness wasn't. The following scriptures refute that line of thinking:

> For everything created by God is good, and nothing is to be rejected, if it is received with gratitude; for it is sanctified by means of the word of God and prayer.
>
> —1 TIMOTHY 4:4–5

> [Fix your hope on] God, who richly supplies us with all things to enjoy.
>
> —1 TIMOTHY 6:17

Many people derive a great deal of joy and happiness from their families. For many, the greatest happiness and joy in life aside from a personal relationship with God are found in family. God does not condemn them for this enjoyment. When it is kept in proper perspective, not made into an idol, God delights in their joy. Obviously, He also delights in giving singles happiness and joy.

Happiness is shaped in part by our attitude toward life, and our attitude is shaped by our beliefs. After resolving the issue about whether or not it is OK to want to be happy and to pursue happiness, the next question to answer is, "From what do I derive my happiness?"

As Christians, we all know the textbook, ironclad answer Jesus. "All my springs of joy are in you, O Lord." (See Psalm 87:7.) God told Abraham that He would be his "exceeding great reward" (Gen. 15:1, KJV). But does this mean that we cannot or should not enjoy *things* in life? What about enjoying a child's laughter, a bright sunny day, a walk at sunset or a card from a dear friend?

Of course it is fine to enjoy these things. When we put it in this simple context, we see the mistake in thinking that there is anything wrong with enjoying life. But somehow, in being single, many of us have developed the mind-set that if God does not want to give us a family, something we so wish to enjoy, then we had better not seek other means of enjoyment either. This simply isn't true.

The next step is really *believing* in your heart that you truly *can* be happy though not married. You can be more than simply "content." You can go beyond that. Much of the struggle to believe this is carried out in your mind. What is your focus? Do you think more about what you *don't* have than about what you *do* have? If so, change your focus. Ponder the joys in your life. Seize those things that bring you joy! Take it in for all it's worth.

Let the pleasures God gives you roll over in your mind. Thank Him. Work at adding the things that bring joy into your week. And dream! Consider all the wide-open possibilities of your future. Nothing is impossible with God. Instead of dreading continuing on your current path, stop. Realize that God is a *big* God. Instead of looking at your future in a negative light, think of the wonders that lie ahead. Joseph suffered heavily for thirteen years, but then he enjoyed the fulfillment of his dream for over seventy years! Abraham and Sarah waited twenty-five heart-wrenching years for Isaac, the fulfillment of their dream. We seem to focus only on the hardship of those years. We don't stop to consider that Sarah then enjoyed her son for twenty-seven years, as did Abraham for seventy-five years! The Bible says Abraham "died in a ripe old age, an old man and *satisfied with life*" (Gen. 25:8, emphasis added).

You just never know what God has in store around the corner for you. Keep dreaming about the countless possibilities of tomorrow instead of viewing tomorrow based on today's narrow lens.

Q **How do I deal with loneliness day after day, perhaps year after year?**

A Much of the material I've read on loneliness has been aimed at short-term loneliness. It assumes that after experiencing a sudden loss, a person goes through a time of adjusting, after which his or her life gets back to *normal*. For me, this type of advice doesn't hit the mark. Much of it runs along the lines of "get active helping others" or "develop a new hobby or area of interest" or "join a club or sign up for a class." All those suggestions are helpful, but I have not found that they have solved my problem over the long haul.

Doing those things doesn't solve the whole problem because the issue goes deeper than just "What am I doing with my time?" or "How much am I getting out with other people?" Loneliness has to be addressed on two levels. One is the surface level that evaluates and makes necessary adjustments aimed only on exterior things such as how and with whom I am spending my time. The other is the deeper level— below the surface. It evaluates, "What am I feeling, and why am I feeling it?"

Let me give you an example from my own life. During weekdays, pressure regarding personal responsibilities would mount, and I'd keep thinking, *The weekend is coming, and I can get things done then.* However, when the weekend came, I would spin my wheels. I'd find myself wishing I could do something with someone in an effort to soothe my loneliness.

Then the tug of war would begin. I would go back and forth asking myself, *Do I have time to try to find someone to do something with, or should I be responsible and get to work on things that need my attention?* By being indecisive, I was ineffective both in getting things done and in getting together with others. This sometimes became a vicious cycle. I tried to deal with my loneliness and also deal with being overwhelmed by all the practical things I had to do. Consequently, I had multiple issues to deal with all at once.

This is often how the devil thwarts our well-being. He plays upon our weaknesses, uses them against us, takes advantage of the poor choices we make in our weak areas and compounds the consequences that hinder us naturally. He heaps things against us to try to overwhelm us so we'll just give in and give up. These problems escalated as long as I continued addressing issues only at the surface level. This is not enough. We must also address issues at a deeper level. When I began doing so, I experienced some real success over loneliness.

Deeper issues provoking loneliness differ for each person, so I cannot address this adequately. But one root issue can involve your ability to feel genuinely *connected* to others. Various issues can hinder or prevent people from being able to connect. Whatever the roots, ask the Lord to show you the deeper-level issues causing your loneliness. Then you must cooperate with Him as He shows you what to do about the root issues.

Accepting and dealing with the fact that sometimes, we just will feel lonely

Our expectations play a large role in how we feel about things. So it is helpful to have realistic expectations regarding loneliness. If you think you should get to the point where you *never* experience loneliness, then you'll likely feel defeated whenever loneliness hits. At the other end of the spectrum, if you resign yourself to feeling lonely as somewhat the norm, then you will miss out on much in life that God wants for you. There is a healthy balance to be found.

The Bible gives principles you can use to overcome loneliness. Loneliness should not be the *norm*. However, the Bible also depicts the fallen nature of the world around us, including our own fallen nature. Consequently, you will experience a certain amount of loneliness. God's *ideal* for you is that you never experience loneliness. But the fact is that you are still dealing with a sin nature and with your own weaknesses and the stresses in your day-to-day life. That means that from time to time you will succumb to loneliness.

You can know that God is with you and feel His presence in a real way. That is wonderful, such a blessing. But even in the midst of feeling God's presence, you may still feel the longing for *the company of people you love*. I believe that God understands this and does not condemn you in it. He doesn't look at you as a "second-class Christian" because you're experiencing this human characteristic that He Himself put within you. When you do feel lonely, don't condemn yourself. Remind yourself that it will pass.

Q **What do I do when I feel that I'd rather be dead than single—when the future, if I remain single, seems to be more than I could possibly bear?**

A You may have battled this kind of thinking. After a teaching I gave to singles, a precious, dear woman came up to me and asked, "Is it all right if I ask God to take my life if He is not going to give me a spouse?" I know others feel as she did. Sometimes pain seems unbearable.

If you find yourself thinking such thoughts, it is so important that you realize where these feelings originate. They come straight from the pit of hell. You have an enemy. His job is to rob, steal and destroy. This is real. The devil is very skilled at producing a "death wish" in you. It doesn't usually happen all at once; otherwise you'd recognize it for what it is and resist it at the onset. Instead it happens by stealth. Bit by bit a person will succumb to despair. Despair turns to hopelessness. Hopelessness turns to death as a supposed escape.

It is no escape—never be tricked into believing it is an escape. Vigorously oppose thoughts and feelings of despair and hopelessness. I find it is helpful to backtrack on my thoughts. How did I get here? What downward spiral of lies did I believe? I need to ask God for discernment and wisdom to start dismantling this downward staircase. Step by step, take it apart. Replace lies with the truth.

The cumulative effect of looking at day after day filled with the same thing you are struggling with today can seem unbearable. But in Matthew 6:34, Jesus said not to worry about tomorrow. He gives us our *daily* bread. We have grace and strength for *today*. There is enough for today. Don't allow yourself to get caught in the trap of worrying that you cannot make it as a single for another year or two or five or ten. Let your focus be on *today*. You *can* get through today. In our weakness, He is made strong.

If you find yourself thinking about death, it is imperative that you seek help immediately. It is humbling to admit these thoughts to another person, but you must. Tell a trusted friend. Tell a leader in your church. Seek professional help if it seems necessary. But do not minimize the significance of these thoughts, not even for a moment. Take them seriously, and take immediate action. Do not walk this out alone. This is why God gives us *people*. During times like these, we are not strong enough to walk alone, and no one requires that of you. God is faithful, and He will give you help directly through Himself and also through His people.

Q **Sometimes I feel like such a "loser" because of how I feel about being single. I feel like I should be able to just get over it. What is wrong with me for having such a hard time not being able to get past how I feel?**

A It is likely that you are dealing with more than you allow yourself to realize. Many of us would prefer just not to think about some of the realities of our lives. It may seem easier to simply ignore the unpleasant aspects. However, if we merely repress our feelings, we don't learn to manage them effectively.

It is not uncommon for many singles to be faced with quite a number of significant challenges. Depending on your unique situation, you may be dealing with a number of things from the following list:

- Longing for a spouse
- Longing for children
- Longing for affection

- Longing for a sense of belonging in the church, where many currently feel out of place
- Losing friends as they marry
- Facing increasing difficulty finding and keeping friends
- Facing intermittent loneliness despite all attempts to combat it
- Feeling misunderstood by couples
- Feeling overlooked by the church leadership
- Feeling like misfits in society
- Fighting the stereotype of singles
- Battling wrong thinking due to twisted theology about singles
- Trying to figure life out on your own with little assistance from others with experience living single
- Struggling to determine appropriate life goals because you are uncertain the future will include a spouse
- Experiencing heartbreaks when serious relationships end
- Unsatisfied sexual desires
- A world turned upside down by divorce and the multitude of issues it brings
- Single parenting
- The death of a spouse

Consider the length of time you have been experiencing any of these challenges. For some, these challenges continue for a very long time—not only for a year or two, but perhaps for ten, twenty or thirty years. *No matter how positive an attitude you have about life, no matter the depth of your spirituality, cumulatively, these experiences create pain.* Anyone who says otherwise is in denial or afraid to admit the truth.

Many of us feel trapped into not admitting our *desires*, let alone our *pain*, even to ourselves. The various admonitions given to singles are too simplistic. They fail to address adequately the complexity of issues singles face. It is critical that you come to a place where you feel free, at least within your own heart, to admit your pain. Sometimes we don't want to admit our pain because we feel that experiencing and admitting pain means we are immature Christians. However, Jesus said that in this world, we would experience *tribulation*. He went on to encourage us by saying, "But take courage; I have overcome the world" (John 16:33). You can overcome through Him. But overcoming does not mean you won't *experience* pain. It means you can learn how to live well in the midst of it. Doing so requires what I refer to as *pain management*.

Unless you become adept at pain management, you may fall off either side of a balance. You may try to deaden your pain, or you may express it too freely, too often. When you get to the point where you can't endure the pain any longer, you will begin to shut down, perhaps becoming sullen. But God does not want you going around half dead. You can learn how to live with your emotions and *face* pain instead of running away from it.

On the other side of the balance, if you don't learn how to manage your pain, unfortunately you may not exercise appropriate discretion with respect to how often and how much of your pain you expose. While getting the pain up and out in the open may be necessary for a *season*, you cannot expect your loved ones to bear that kind of burden indefinitely. It wears them out. Yes, we all are to "bear one another's burdens" (Gal. 6:2), but there comes a point where we can overburden others if we constantly expose our pain. The right way to deal with this is to share it with Jesus, the ultimate burden bearer, and learn how to carry it with God's grace and enabling power.

By touching on this subject, I hope I've opened the door for you to admit your pain and seek tools to manage it properly. I can't adequately cover the subject of pain management here, but I'd like to highlight a few common elements of a plan that, although not specialized, likely will be helpful to everyone.

The elements of this plan include worship, prayer and Bible reading. Another common element for most people, perhaps more so for women, is to talk with someone who isn't threatened by the need or depth of pain. Use wisdom in this. For example, it isn't a good idea always to go to the same person. It can become too much for one friend to bear, no matter how great a friend he or she is. Although you might have one person who seems to be able to comfort you better than anyone, you shouldn't turn constantly to that same person. Your relationship will be healthier and stronger for it.

Your plan could also include practical elements like recreation, engaging in a home project, surprising a friend with a blessing or something else that lifts your spirits and recharges your emotional battery. Managing pain is draining. You can't expect to look beyond yourself as a way to address it *all* the time. Sure, it's good to take your eyes off yourself and give to others in greater need. But when your cup is empty—and for singles, this can happen pretty quickly due to a lack of companionship—you have to act responsibly and do things that fill your tank. That is not being selfish and self-centered; that is using good sense and taking proper care of your emotional and spiritual well-being. "Watch over your heart with *all diligence*, for from it flow the springs of life" (Prov. 4:23, emphasis added).

Chapter 4

Pursuing Marriage

Q What is the balance between not idolizing the idea of getting married and having a sincere desire to be married?

A To answer this question, let's examine Matthew 5:29–30. If someone is struggling against the temptation to lust or commit adultery, Jesus teaches: "If your right eye makes you stumble, tear it out...if your right hand makes you stumble, cut it off." Well, is there something intrinsically wrong with our eye or hand? No. But aspects of our natural human traits and attributes *can* become problematic for us, and if they do, Jesus is telling us to deal with it, and be ruthless about it!

Similarly, the desire to be married is not wrong in and of itself, but it is a problem if it becomes an idol. (An idol is anything in our lives we desire or value more than God.) So how do we know if it is? As with any issue concerning possible sin, your starting point is to ask the Holy Spirit to convict you. The Bible says, "The heart is more deceitful than all else and is desperately sick; who can understand it?" (Jer. 17:9). Paul said he could not evaluate himself, but instead he relied on God to reveal sin to him (1 Cor. 4:4). David asked God to search his heart (Ps. 139:23–24). In John 16:8 we see that it is the Holy Spirit's job to convict us of sin. So that's your starting point—asking God to show you if, in fact, the desire for marriage has risen to the point of idolatry.

What are some of the signs that it has risen that far? Well, does it control you? Are most of your decisions formed on the basis of achieving this goal? For example, is that the sole factor guiding you in deciding what church to attend, irrespective of

God's leading? Do you bounce around various home groups for that purpose alone? Is that the measuring stick for how you will involve yourself in ministry in the church? Do you compromise your values to achieve that goal? The point is this: Does your desire to be married *drive* you? If it does, then in all likelihood, it is idolatry, and you must deal with it.

You are breaking God's heart. He jealously desires your love and devotion, and you are turning away from Him by seeking someone above Him. Ultimately, that idol not only breaks God's heart, but it also will break your own. It will drive you to make decisions you will later regret. Perhaps you will marry for the wrong reasons, only later to discover the problems that creep up as a result of your initial faulty motivations. Be ruthless, and renounce the idolatry. Expect this to be excruciatingly painful. It will be. But the good news is that the fruit of repentance is sweet (Heb. 12:11). And the freedom that comes from letting go of idols is likewise wonderful. Recommit your whole self to God once again.

Conversely, God does not want us weighed down by false guilt if, in fact, we truly are not idolizing marriage but simply have a genuine, healthy desire for it. It is not a sin to want to be married! This should be obvious! But because of the bad advice that gets passed around, this needs to be stated outright. Consider all the people who are married; they must have wanted to get married, right?

If you have been single for any length of time, wrong assumptions are sometimes made about your desires. People may suggest that you are idolizing marriage or are disobeying God by not relinquishing that desire. Usually the people who propose this really love us. After all, it takes courage to confront someone about a potential sin issue. And for those for whom it truly is a sin issue, thank God for people who are willing to bring this challenge. However, we must not let the fact of this challenge confuse the real issues. In other words, don't allow the challenge to become synonymous with guilt.

Just because someone brings up this issue, don't jump to the conclusion that any desire you have for marriage must be wrong. Allow God to search your heart and bring it in balance if anything is off balance.

Sometimes the extreme pain we can feel in not being married gets confused with the issue of idolatry. Just because you feel an extreme amount of pain—perhaps the pain of loneliness, for an extended time—this does not mean that marriage is an idol in your life. You are just feeling a lot of pain. It can be that simple. You have a healthy, normal desire that is not being met. That's painful—sometimes extremely painful. But that does not mean your desire is an idol.

To be balanced at these times, you need to press into God for grace that the desire for marriage does not become an idol. When you are in a lot of pain, you are at a weak point. That's when you are more susceptible to caving into temptations—and one temptation can be to turn marriage into an idol. In an effort to soothe your pain, you may be tempted to chase after this idol to make things better. At these times, you have to discipline yourself to run to God. He promises to help you. And He does.

Q **What is wrong with the teaching that you must lay down your desire to marry before God will give you a spouse?**

A It is erroneous theologically to say that all singles across the board must totally relinquish their desire for marriage before God will give them a spouse. Advising a single that he or she must first relinquish this desire presupposes one of two things:

1. The person has made an idol of the desire to be married and has a need to repent.

2. God has spoken to the person and specifically required him or her to lay it down, much as He called Abraham to sacrifice Isaac.

If either of these presumptions *is* true of you, obedience to God is required, not so that God will bring a spouse, but because we owe Him our allegiance. Each of us—married and single—needs to submit our life fully to God. This is what it means to proclaim Jesus as Lord over your life. (See Luke 6:46; John 14:23–24.) Consequently, if a desire is idolatrous, you must repent. If God requires the desire to be sacrificed, you must obey.

This type of counsel is sound, but a problem arises when people *assume* that merely because a single strongly desires to be married, the desire is idolatrous. Or they *assume* God has required the sacrificing of that desire.

Yes, it is right to caution singles against idolatry. Sometimes it is a problem, but not always. The desire to marry can be quite strong for all the reasons I describe later regarding marriage and its accoutrements. Consequently, it can be confused with idolatry. It is important that we discern the difference between natural, normal, healthy, strong desires and idolatry, because if we do not discern rightly, we lay an unnecessary and harmful burden on singles.

Regarding the issue of sacrifice, while it is always good to encourage obedience, it can be harmful to imply that a person is disobeying God by not relinquishing (sacrificing) a desire if, in fact, God has not required this. God does not ask *everyone* who has a desire for something to lay down that desire. While He does want all of our desires to be yielded and submitted to Him, that does not mean that all desires are bad, out of control or unyielded. You may have a desire for marriage that is God-given, normal and healthy. It may be yielded, submitted and in its proper perspective. God had His specific purposes for testing Abraham's heart when He called him to sacrifice Isaac. He may indeed decide to test your allegiance, but you must be careful not to wrongly presume that is what God is doing when it is not.

A testimony relative to dying to the desire to marry is

common among singles. We've all heard it. The newly engaged person explains, "Well, I *finally* got to the point where I *sincerely* told God that it was OK if He never gave me a spouse, and right after that, my fiancé walked into my life!"

So, after hearing this testimony often, we assume, "That's my problem, and there's my solution." It becomes almost like a formula—do *this*, and God will do *that*. But it doesn't work like that. We can't put God in a box. And God wants to spare us from the disappointment of mistaken presumption.

Q **Is it OK to pray fervently for God to bring a spouse into my life?**

A Yes! The Bible says this in Philippians 4:6–7 (emphasis added):

> Be anxious for nothing, but in everything by prayer
> and supplication with thanksgiving *let your requests be
> made known to God*. And the peace of God, which sur-
> passes all comprehension, shall guard your hearts and
> your minds in Christ Jesus.

God is our heavenly Father, and He welcomes our requests! But we need to make our requests appropriately. All of us have witnessed a child ask a parent for something in a right way and a wrong way. There is a demanding, whining way and a respectful, peaceable way. The approach is formed by the child's attitude about himself or herself in relation to the parent. One child may be self-centered or may mistrust the parent's good intentions, while another child may respect his or her parent's authority and trust in the parent's heart of love in either granting or denying the request.

We too have to examine our attitudes about ourselves and toward God in discerning whether it is OK to ask God to bring a spouse into our lives. Let's look at a great example in the Bible of a woman who prayed about her unmet desire—Hannah (1 Sam. 1:8–20). She deeply desired to have a child. She prayed in earnest. God granted her the desire of her heart. We see no evidence of God disdaining her earnest plea.

I think the reason we even question whether it is OK to ask God for a spouse is because we are very concerned about whether it is OK with God that we *want* a spouse. We think, *After all, if God has not given me a spouse, I guess He just doesn't want me to be married yet. So I shouldn't ask. When it is His time, He will bring it about. I need to wait patiently, not ask, and thereby prove my acceptance of His will.* Well, that is a very noble attitude. Certainly God loves that kind of humility and submission. But in that same humility and submission we can pray for a spouse.

I don't pretend to understand how prayer works or why God chooses to use the vehicle of prayer to change events on this earth as He does. But clearly, He does. Recently, I joined many people in praying for a woman who was in a coma and not expected to live. The prediction was death, but God intervened, and she is alive today. All of us can think of countless examples when everything seemed headed in a certain direction. Then people prayed, and things changed. If you have a desire to be married and nothing is happening, pray. Yes, do pray.

Psalm 37:4 says, "Delight yourself in the Lord; and He will give you the desires of your heart." Thus, I believe God would take away my desire to be married if He wanted to. Because He has allowed the desire to remain, all the more I take this as an indication that I should continue asking.

Q **How active should I be in the process of finding a spouse? Is it all God's doing? If I take any role in it at all, does that mean I am not trusting God? When is it like "birthing an Ishmael" for me to get involved in the process?**

A There is both an appropriate and inappropriate amount of time and energy to give toward achieving any goal we set for our lives. What those amounts are depends upon who you are and the call of God on your life. The bottom line is that you have to be convinced in your own mind and heart about what God is directing you to do, and be as clear as possible about what is your responsibility and what is His (Rom. 14:22). God requires some people to put much effort into finding a spouse. For others, He seems to just drop one in their lap. He alone knows the plans He has for you, so seek His guidance.

Let's look at some practical examples. When I moved to Ohio, I needed a job. I put much hard work into finding employment. I did not assume a job was going to just fall in my lap simply because I *needed* a job. I asked God to open the right doors and to shut the wrong doors. I trusted God for favor, connections and every other need every step of the way. In other words, I trusted God to work actively on my behalf and do things for me that I could not do for myself. But I also had to be active. I needed to act responsibly and do the normal things one does when looking for work.

The same principle applied when I started looking for a house. It took work, time and faith. I trusted God to lead me to the right house. With respect to many other goals in my life, there has been a mixture of God working, me looking to Him and trusting Him, and also, me taking *action* in conjunction with exercising faith and trusting in Him. We see a biblical basis for this approach in the account of God bringing together Ruth and Boaz. Does Satan deceive some of us whom God *is* calling to action into thinking that this is one area where we can just be passive and watch it fall into our laps?

On the other hand, I know people whom God instructed simply to continue doing the things to which He had called them. They had an assurance from God that meeting a spouse would just happen. For some, it has. Psalm 37:23 says, "The steps of a good man are ordered by the LORD; and he delighteth in his way" (KJV). Proverbs 3:5–6 says, "Trust in the LORD with all your heart, and do not lean on your own understanding. In all your ways, acknowledge Him, and He will make your paths straight." Certainly, for many people, God simply puts them in the right place at the right time. We see this in the account of God providing a bride for Isaac (Gen. 24).

For those who do actively seek a spouse, when are we going too far? When are we taking matters into our own hands and thus "birthing an Ishmael"? (Ishmael was the son born to Abraham through his wife's maid. God promised Abraham he'd become the father of many nations, but after a long wait, he and his wife Sarah decided to bring about God's promise in the way *they* thought best.) First, do you have a promise regarding marriage like the promise Abraham had about a son? If yes, then you must patiently wait until God brings the fulfillment. Do your part, but keep your heart soft toward God, even in a long wait. You are going too far when you get impatient and try to force things to happen by your own doing. The bottom line is, seek, trust and obey God.

Q If I do actively try to find a spouse, what avenues are OK to use? Is it OK to use a dating service? May I change churches in order to find a mate? Should I limit myself to dating only people referred to me by people I trust?

A I don't think the process itself is nearly as important as the attitude of your heart in the pursuit. We can be very vigorous, even to the point of attending another church, if we truly believe in our hearts that it is *God* leading us to make that decision. As for dating services vs. limiting ourselves to dating only those referred to us—you have to pray and use common sense. A lot also depends on how much of a risk taker you are.

Whatever you do, your heart must be in the right place—submitted to God and looking to Him throughout every step in the process. The more aggressive you are, the more you need to guard your heart, making sure that you are not deceiving yourself. You may be letting the search begin to rule you instead of allowing God to rule in your life. It is good to discuss your approach and attitudes with wise and trusted friends who know you well and who will hold you accountable if it seems that you are going too far. You need to make a commitment to weigh carefully what they tell you, should they in fact confront you.

Q **When I do date someone, how do I deal with all the scrutiny of my family and friends regarding my decisions, especially a decision to end a relationship? How do I resist the pressure, real or perceived, caused by feeling that people think at this age that if someone is interested, I should find a way to make it work? How do I handle my concerns that if I end a relationship, they will think there's something wrong with me…that I'm being too picky or something else?**

A Ultimately, this is where we are tested to stand by our principles and choices, and to stand up to scrutiny. Relationships are not cut and dry, and we can't expect people not to formulate their own opinions about our choices. What often complicates matters further is when you have made a quality decision to surround yourself with true friends whom you trust to speak truth into your life even when you may not want to hear it—and they do—and you disagree with it. We have to be willing to receive and sort through the input and advice others give us. It's true that many times others who are not directly involved in a situation have clearer eyes to see what needs to be seen. So we need to stay open to receiving what others whom we trust have to say.

At the same time, we answer to God, so His view is the one that truly counts. We must earnestly, sincerely seek God for

His direction and wisdom in every situation. As mentioned earlier, at some point, we have to take a step of faith believing that we've received the guidance we need from God. If our hearts are in the right place, God will be faithful to head us in the right direction on difficult and weighty decisions such as getting engaged or breaking off a relationship. I believe this is true even if we initially start heading in the wrong direction. If we genuinely want to follow and obey God, He'll be faithful to turn us when needed and keep us on His path. (See Psalm 37:5, 23; Proverbs 16:3, 9; 20:24; Jeremiah 10:23.)

If we maintain this posture toward God and make decisions as best we can from that posture, then what others think cannot hold sway over us. When others disagree with our decision, we simply must develop "thick skin" and move ahead despite what we know they think of our choice. We will live with the good fruit of good decisions or the consequences of bad decisions.

We should not make decisions based on a desire to please people. Respect them, yes. Thank them for their input. State your gratitude for their willingness to be honest with you and say what may have been very difficult to say. Affirm them for being the kinds of friends whose wounds are "faithful" (Prov. 27:6). Then, graciously, tactfully, explain the decision you've made and the reasons why.

Do you owe them an explanation? Many times I think people assume they do not, because, after all, "It's my life and my choice." But we are not islands. Our lives touch and affect others. Because of this, we do "owe" them some sort of explanation. We may not need to give all the details, but if we will at least give basic information, this honors those who are willing to step in and say something uncomfortable. Doing this also reinforces a wide-open door in the future. When they see that you handled their input maturely, they will stay open to giving you input in the future. And we all need this throughout life. We have our blind spots, and we do need others to see things for us at times that we are incapable of seeing.

Chapter 5

Walking in the Freedom of Truth

Q Why do I feel as if there is something wrong with me when I honestly believe I'm a normal, emotionally healthy person?

A More than likely, the answer is because you are under the cloud of the stereotype. An unfortunate consequence of the lack of teaching about singles to the whole church is the perpetuation of stereotypes about singles. We can't afford to make light of the existence of these stereotypes or pretend they're not there. When people allow stereotypes to persist in their thinking, it's as if they throw a cloak on a person and form opinions based solely on the stereotype. We even do this to ourselves and other singles! Although we have left behind the stereotypes engendered by the terms "spinster" and "old maid," other negative stereotypes persist.

There seems to be an assumption in the church that a single person is somewhat emotionally unhealthy or broken. This stereotype cripples us needlessly. Let me illustrate the falsity of this stereotype and hopefully be a tool God uses to obliterate it by telling you a bit of my own story. I lay this out not to call attention to my accomplishments, but only because I believe God wants to use it to smash the stereotypes and the typical mind-sets about why a person is still single. I also think you will relate to much of my story. After this, we'll see why it's so important to straighten out our thinking relative to stereotypes.

Regularly, people say to me things such as, "Why are *you* still single?" or "I just can't believe you are still single!" I've even had people literally cock their head, furrow their brow and say, "I just *reeeeeeally* don't get it." I know these comments were actually compliments, but in the back of my mind, I'd find myself wondering, *So what conclusions are they making about me now? They're thinking there surely must be something wrong with me, or else I'd be married. They're wondering what the deep hidden flaw is.* I'd find myself wanting to come back with some response—something…anything that would convince them that I really was *normal*. But that's not possible. In those times, we have to hand our reputation and self-image over to Jesus, even though we wish we weren't even in a position to have to hand anything over.

As for the questions people posed, well, I don't know why I'm still single either. But it's not because there was something so terribly wrong with me. There were several marriage opportunities, but after earnest prayer, none culminated in marriage. So, as you read my story, focus on all the opportunities there were for me to meet Mr. Right (not Mr. Perfect—just Mr. Right).

I hope you'll recognize that I was just a "normal," American girl. I think you too will be confounded as to *why* I am still single. I pray that God will use my story to open the eyes of many people to understand that there are *lots* of other singles who are just like me—normal, healthy, successful individuals who, for reasons unbeknownst to them, still find themselves single. Additionally, I pray that many people will come to understand why it is so important that we destroy the stereotypes and unshackle those who are in bondage because of them.

MY STORY

I attended Boca Raton Community High School in Boca Raton, Florida. It was a very large school; my graduating class was almost six hundred. (Lots of fish in that pond.) I was very active in school. I also had quite a variety of friends. I had two older brothers, who also were well known and well liked. You would think with *two older brothers* (one who was two grades ahead, and the other, three) that I was perfectly set up, right?

I also was very active in my church. I was an officer of my parish's Catholic Youth Organization, and I went on to be elected as an officer for the entire archdiocese, which spanned from West Palm Beach all the way to Miami, Florida. I attended annual conventions and even was chosen "Queen" one year. In summary, I was well known and well connected, not just in my hometown, but also in the Catholic Church on the whole east coast of South Florida. In particular, I had close ties to a number of guys in an *all boys* Catholic high school near Ft. Lauderdale. In fact, I dated a few guys from there, including one of the leading student government officers. I'm pretty certain that I attended more proms and "senior nights" than any of my friends. However, no relationship bloomed that carried me into my college years.

I attended the University of Florida, a university with a very large student body. I hoped that I would meet my future husband there. I was an active member of a sorority, and, for a time, I dated the president of one of the fraternities. Well, I didn't meet my husband in college, but in my senior year, I dedicated my life fully to God, and the spiritual aspect of my life really started soaring like never before.

I then became part of a nationwide campus ministry, so there were lots of wonderful Christian men that I was with frequently. I even worked and lived in the ministry's "staff house," so I had lots of interaction with my male peers. I joined the full-time staff of this ministry after graduating. I was in a high-profile position and the only female on staff. Because of my position, I was well known in our ministry's region. To top that off, I was actually fairly prominent in the ministry nationwide. I attended national conferences yearly where I met lots of men from around the country. And *still*, nothing evolved toward marriage!

Now, come on—are you getting the picture here? I mean,

I really loved Jesus with all my heart, and people considered me to be intelligent and articulate, poised and self-confident, well liked and attractive. I don't say this to flatter myself, but just to explain that it wasn't like I was a wallflower hiding in a corner somewhere with no chance to meet wonderful Christian men! I even loved a lot of outdoor recreational activities, similar to my male friends, like hiking, camping, biking, racquetball and sailing. Still, Mr. Right never entered the picture.

When I was twenty-seven, I felt God directing me to attend graduate school at Regent University in Virginia Beach, Virginia. I wasn't going for the purpose of finding a spouse—I truly felt God was calling me there—but, as you can imagine, it was on my mind! And what better place to find a husband than at a Christian graduate school, linked to a major international ministry (Christian Broadcasting Network), where I'd meet like-minded individuals? But I didn't find my man at Regent, either.

I moved to Columbus, Ohio, when I was thirty-one, quickly became a member of Vineyard Church of Columbus, and made new friends. At that time the church membership was around five hundred people. Now, thirteen years later, we are up over six thousand. So there are a lot of fish in this pond, too. I've definitely been active and "visible" in my church. I even spoke to the *entire* congregation once, and the pastor jokingly said he was going to have my telephone number flash up on the screen. Still, nothing has happened.

I've also had a great job working for the Ohio legislature for the last thirteen years. I'm "visible" there, too. I staff a standing committee of the Senate, and my job requires a lot of interaction with legislators, their aides, lobbyists, legislative liaisons of various executive branch state agencies, as well as the staff of my own agency.

Despite all these opportunities, I simply have not met the right person to marry. And by that one fact alone, I have had

the cloak thrown over me, and who I really am doesn't matter
at that point. I'm single, so it must mean there's something
wrong with me. Period. Sure, people don't come right out and
say it, but people do think it. And we singles know they do. It's
a horrible cloud to have to walk under.

PLAGUED WITH THE STEREOTYPE

Unfortunately, I think you can relate to how awful this is as I
describe what it did to me. If you can relate, I hope it comforts
you to know you're not crazy! Others have experienced this,
too. Here I was, so vibrant in my youth—a leader, a "go-getter"
from a household of go-getters. Our home was always a happening place for as long as I can remember. I was used to being
in the spotlight—in the right kind of way—where you're trying
to lead people down a good path.

I had a picture of myself as being a great mom and a
devoted wife. I wanted my home to be like the one I grew up
in—a hub of the neighborhood and strong support to the
church. But instead, I had this shroud over me. It might as
well have been on my forehead: "I'm single; I'm a loser." (If
you think I'm going too far, consider this line from the movie
The Kid: "So I'm forty, I don't have a dog, and I'm not married. I grow up to be a loser.")

Yet, I had a picture of who I was as a person. I *knew* who I
was. But the longer I remained single, the more I came under
the stereotypic negative image. And please realize, that negative image is the *exact opposite* of who I saw myself to be. It can
be almost maddening to *know* you are one way, but to feel the
world telling you something very different. Before long you
wonder if you do, in fact, match that negative image that is
portrayed. It is hard to put words to, but this facet of what singles go through has been one of the hardest, if not *the* hardest
aspect for me. It's one thing to slowly watch the hopes and
dreams you held for your life melt away, but it is compounded
exponentially when you can't seem to get out from underneath

a negative image that totally misrepresents everything about you. Only by the grace of God have I not caved into it.

TEACHING THAT REINFORCES THE STEREOTYPE

This stereotype is reinforced by the subject matter most available for singles—the topics of books or teachings most often targeted to us. These past twenty-five years, most of the teaching I have heard aimed at singles seems to fall basically into three categories: healthy dating, sexual purity and overcoming social ineptitude. I call these the "big three." Constant repetition of these three themes to the exclusion of other more varied issues perpetuates an unhealthy caricature of singles.

Yes, some of us do need to learn more about these issues. But when the *majority* of teaching aimed at the single population hits on these three themes repeatedly, it sends a message that *all* singles deal with these issues *regularly*. This in turn sends a message, to both couples and singles, that singles generally are immature or unhealthy. This can shroud singles under an unhealthy cloak of shame, and it strengthens the stereotype. For the singles who do need help in those areas, it is demeaning to always be served the same thing. For singles who do not need help in those areas, it is repulsive.

Think about this for a moment. If you have heard a message to singles, did it address only the subject of dating and sexual purity? Or perhaps did it address issues concerning "typical" problems assumed to be causes for remaining single? For example, did it suggest that men over thirty haven't married because they can't commit, or that older women are still single because their expectations are too high? The scope of these issues is far too narrow. Are these issues important? Yes. Should they be discussed? Of course. But we also need teaching that addresses the everyday challenges of singles.

As an aside, this repeated teaching is egregious not only because it reinforces the stereotype, but also because the "big three" are not necessarily the biggest issues we face. Many singles are not dating regularly, and when we do, many feel adept at it—many know *how* to date. Sexual temptation is an issue, and it always will be. But that doesn't mean we have to focus on it *all the time*. In fact, too much focus on it can create problems that weren't there before! (What are we feeding our minds?) My single female friends don't place this at the top of their list of woes; not even close. I've had far more couples suggest it to be the top problem of singles than singles themselves. Apparently my experience reflects the norm. In a national survey given both to singles and *couples*, singles ranked feeling left out as their number one problem, while sexual frustration was fifth. *Couples* perceived the number one problem of singles to be sexual frustration.[1]

Many singles are emotionally healthy, stable, socially adept individuals. Just like the population at large, many are attractive and intelligent. There are countless reasons why singles are single, and many reasons have nothing to do with brokenness. People really dishonor singles when they teach that the typical reason singles are not married is because there's something "wrong" with them. Number one...there's something "wrong" with all of us, and that doesn't prevent God from bringing people together in marriage. Number two, it is simply unreasonable to characterize half the population as being too "broken" to be married.

LAYING THE AX AT THE ROOT

We need to smash the stereotypes through better teaching that is given to the whole church about singles. The more truth people have about singles, the more we will be able to eliminate the stereotypes and end the bondages they bring. My hope, as you'll read later, is that pastors will begin teaching more frequently and accurately on subjects concerning the single life. This will go a long way in smashing the stereotypes. You too play a role. Hand this book out to help people see many truths that will eliminate stereotypes. Let your life reflect the fallacy of these stereotypes. When comments borne out of these stereotypes are spoken in your presence, lovingly and tactfully explain the erroneous thinking that spurred the comment. If the comment angered or hurt you, and in that moment you cannot speak out of love, it is best to remain silent. If you offend while trying to correct someone, then the cycle of hurt just continues. Additionally, your correction will be hard to receive and thus will be ineffective.

THROW OFF THAT CLOAK!

The Lord certainly does not see you through the eyes of that stereotype, so neither should you. Work to throw off the cloak that shrouds you under the shame of the stereotype! Make a decision to walk free from it. Ask God to give you eyes to see ways you may have unconsciously succumbed to thinking of yourself consistent with the stereotype. Pull out the sword of the Spirit, which is the Word of God, and align yourself with what God's Word says about you. That is the truth. That's what sets us free. That's what matters.

Q Can I be content and still have a desire to marry, or does being content mean I've relinquished this desire? Is contentment an "all or nothing" proposition, or can we experience it in degrees?

A Desire and contentment are related topics, but distinctly different. However, they often get intertwined, which causes confusion in some key ways.

Being content does not equate to saying, "I have no desire to marry." This is important to understand, because it is easy for people to invert those two concepts so that being discontented is equated with saying, "I desire to marry." And since we know that discontentment is a negative thing, then that puts *desire* in a *negative* light, as if there is something wrong with desiring to marry. This trips us up, making us feel as if we have to die to our desire in order to achieve contentment. Sitting there reading this in black and white, you may readily realize how ridiculous this twisted concept is, but unfortunately, this view definitely is projected to us. We have to realize that a person can be content and simultaneously desire to marry. These don't cancel each other out.

We all live on a continuum between being very content and very discontented. While we may generally stay near a fixed point during our various seasons of growth and maturation, all along the way we are bound to experience ebbs and flows in our level of contentment. (All of us, married and single, experience this in our areas of desire.)

Various factors influence this. For example, I've had instances where, within a short time, several friends got engaged, married, had babies or some combination of these life events. When these types of things happen in close succession, it's more challenging to stay content. At times like these, I may become very discontented and desperately want to marry. I can feel like screaming, "Don't teach me how to cope with it; I just want out!"

There are other times when I can say, as Paul said in Philippians 4:11, "I have learned to be content in whatever circumstances I am." Yes, I'd love to marry, but I am OK being single. There is a submitted, quiet calm in my heart as I trust God, like Paul, to "do all things," even live a content single life, "through Him who strengthens me" (Phil. 4:13).

One of the main reasons we drift on the continuum is due to the tension between desire and contentment. These have to be kept in balance, and that is not always easy because desire wants to swallow up contentment! Sustaining the right balance requires maturity, and sometimes, maturity is gained by falling off balance and working to regain it. After all, Paul did say, "I have *learned* to be content." It isn't automatic; it's a learned process.

Christian singles know that we're *supposed* to live on the contentment end of the continuum. That's the goal. That's the ideal, and we *know* it. So when asked if we are content, we may likely feel *compelled* to say we are because we know this is the "right" answer. However, in all honesty, we might actually be uncertain about whether we are content *enough*, especially in light of all the confusion about this topic. We may wonder if we are pleasing God. Our answer lies in Philippians 3:12–16 where Paul tells us that although we've not laid hold of perfection, we should press on and peacefully trust that God will (uncondemningly) show us where we're off the mark. As with many things in the Christian life, we are striving toward what we know to be the right goal, yet in reality, we are not always there. However, if God is not condemning us, let's not condemn one another. Let's encourage and inspire one another instead!

Q **Is it true that singles have a lot of free time? Why don't I feel that way?**

A A common misconception held about singles (other than single parents) is that we have lots of free time, in stark contrast to couples. Yet a single bears the full responsibility for his or her home, finances, car, yard, repairs, cleaning, shopping, meal preparation and so on *alone* unless some of these responsibilities are shared with roommates. True, singles without children do not bear the added responsibilities that children bring, but commonly they do not *share any* responsibilities with another. This makes a *big* difference that is often overlooked. This fact is not, however, overlooked by the authors of *The Case for Marriage*. They discuss this struggle and pointedly state the distinct advantages couples enjoy with respect to shared obligations.[2] Additionally, many couples enjoy the benefits of sharing obligations for a season both before and after they have children under their roof.

Thus, they may be able to accomplish jointly far more in those seasons than a single can.

The lives of many singles are no less "busy" than that of married people. The time needed to take care of responsibilities can easily be no less, and may even be more for a single than for a married person. Let's do away with this faulty generalization.

I think people get the impression singles have a lot of spare time because when invited to join others in an event, some singles can pretty readily answer *yes*, which may seem quite different from the common response of a married person. This can happen for several reasons. A single doesn't need to check with a spouse before committing to something. Also, a single with no children doesn't have to check the master calendar of the entire family to make sure there are no conflicts. If a single doesn't have a lot of social opportunities *constantly* scheduled, that single may be more highly motivated for a get-together than a married person just because of the difference in social needs between singles and couples. Additionally, even if you are quite busy, you may have flexibility to shift responsibilities to an alternate time. If a social opportunity comes up during a time I had planned on taking care of a personal responsibility, I can find a different time for that. So what is perceived to be more time on the part of singles actually may be only more control over the schedule.

Q **Is it true that it is easier for singles to go out on the mission field? What's wrong with this teaching?**

A Many of us have heard the teaching that it is easier for singles to go out on the mission field than it is for couples. First, we all, married and single, should follow God's leading—that's how decisions regarding mission work should be determined. With that as a given, let's take a closer look at this teaching. Why do we *think* it's easier for singles? I believe the primary reason is because many singles don't have children, so this is presumed to make going on the mission field less complicated. The lives of singles in contrast to families are perceived to be less complicated generally.

Even if both of these perceptions are true for a single (and for some singles, the "less complicated" part is *not* true), this does not mean that going is *easier*. Both couples and singles must make sacrifices, albeit different ones. Singles have to leave behind their closest support system, unlike families who take theirs with them! Once on the field, singles still have to face all the same feelings about being single. Even with the satisfaction and joy that comes from obeying God, being overseas does not somehow alleviate those feelings. And on the field, singles may have less people to whom they can comfortably express those feelings. From a purely practical standpoint, by leaving, singles further diminish the possibility of marriage, especially with an American. Additionally, many cultures are more family-centric than our American culture, so a single feels more like an anomaly in those cultures. Not only is this hard emotionally, but it may be harder for singles in those cultures to gain credibility with the people to whom they are reaching out.

As for the "free" part—this is more a function of life circumstances than it is marital status. For example, as a single you may be caring for an elderly parent, may own a home or may be the executive officer of a large corporation. The variables are endless.

I have a dear single friend who was on the mission field for years. Contrary to all the notions about how much easier it is for singles to be on the mission field, this friend experienced increasing difficulty precisely because of being single. It was noticeably harder for her than the families on her team. Eventually, she felt released to leave the field. Her chief relief was coming out from under the heightened pressures she faced specifically because she was single.

Another single missionary I know has told me of the challenges and difficulties she has experienced specifically because she is single. She personally testifies to the hardships I described above. She experiences the challenges I describe in this book, even in a totally different culture.

Let's do away with the faulty generalization that it is easier for singles to go out on the mission field.

Chapter 6

Issues Involving Married Friends

Q How do I avoid envy when my friends get married, have children, enjoy holidays, enjoy vacations and enjoy life generally? How do I remain truly happy for the blessings God bestows on them? Why is it critical to convey to them the genuine joy I experience for them over their blessings?

A We all can relate to being in a situation where we were able to do something enjoyable that a friend had to miss out on, right? And when you talk about it after the fact, what do you jokingly say to your friend—"Oh, it was awful; you didn't miss a thing!" Right? We want to downplay it because we don't want our friend to feel badly. And yet, if it was really important to us, isn't there a part of us that wants to explain the experience—to share it?

Well, these kinds of things come and go in life. They are not that big of a deal in and of themselves. But when this type of experience is repeated day after day, it's a different story. It becomes a big deal.

A significant part of relating is sharing life experiences. If my married friends get to the point where they feel they cannot share the joys of their lives with me because they fear it will hurt too much in reminding me of what I don't have, the friendship will not thrive. It may even die. So it is of utmost importance that the door stays open when it comes to sharing joys. My inward response to their good news varies. Sometimes I am completely happy for them, without a thought of contrast to my own life. Other times I'm happy for them but find it difficult not to contrast.

Many factors contribute to my inward response. When their news triggers personal sadness, I have to take that to God and let Him minister to me about it. It is best not to disclose this struggle to the friend whose news triggered the feelings. I pray, saying, "God, please enable me to handle this." This prayer must be mixed with faith believing He *will* do it, otherwise we walk off in disbelief and never expect God to come through—which doesn't mean He won't, but it does mean we'll likely not recognize His answer. There is a big difference between a prayer where we merely spill our emotions only in an attempt to relieve ourselves vs. a prayer made in faith that God cares, is listening and will respond.

This doesn't mean that I never discuss my struggles over things of this nature with my married friends. I do, because this too is a significant part of relating. I talk about the subject in general, not about their experiences specifically. I do so not at the time they are relating their good news, but at some other time. If I feel an intense need to talk to *someone* about a specific trigger, I choose a trusted friend other than the one whose news triggered my feelings. This is just using wisdom in relationships generally.

In all of these types of situations, it helps to remember the words of 2 Corinthians 10:12, which says that when we compare ourselves with others, we are "without understanding." My life is blessed in ways that others' lives are not. We must remember that God is loving, and He is also just. There are many inequities in this life that we cannot understand. God sees everything, though, and He is in control. When it's all said and done, ultimately we all will recognize God's supreme wisdom in all His sovereign acts (Isa. 41:21–24).

 How do I become a significant person to the children of my married friends? What if I don't want to be, or what if I don't like their children?

Ask the parents of the children for advice. They know their children best. A child's age, personality and temperament dictate much about which approaches are effective. The most important ingredient you need is love. Love will guide you with respect to many things, but practical pointers are also needed. Parents have to learn a lot about raising children in order to do it well. They understand that we can't rely solely on intuition or instinct. So don't be embarrassed to ask. They will not think you are foolish for asking! Instead, they will be blessed that you care enough to seek the right information.

If you don't care to be a significant person to the children, it may be because your friendship with that particular family is not going to be very deep. It may be sweet, but not terribly deep. Or your friendship may wind up being primarily only with one spouse, and not truly with the entire family. There's nothing wrong in either case. Friendships come in all "shapes and sizes."

If, however, you do feel drawn to have a good friendship with a family, but find you are not particularly fond of one or two of the children, all is not lost! God can do remarkable things if you just ask Him. You've probably experienced situations in the past where you asked God to change your heart toward someone, and He did! Perhaps you experienced this with a coworker, neighbor or member of your home group. Do the same in this instance. Then watch God work on your heart. Be open to change. You'll be blessed to see how God turns your distaste into fond affection.

Q **How do I overcome feeling like a misfit or oddball when so many things in life generally and in my church specifically are geared toward couples or families?**

A Well, practically all of Part II addresses this in one way or another. Obviously I believe God is in the midst of changing cultural mind-sets so that singles won't feel like misfits or oddballs. In the meantime, as He works, there are things we can do to guard ourselves from succumbing to this negative view of ourselves. The simple truth is that we are *not* oddballs. We must do whatever we can do to "[renew] our minds" by the "washing of water with the word" (Rom. 12:2; Eph. 5:26). We must tell ourselves what God's Word says about ourselves over and over until it is so firmly rooted in us that it is sufficient to quell all the messages that try to tell us we are misfits. There are countless scriptures telling us who we are in Christ, but you would do well to write out scriptures that really minister this truth to you; read them regularly. I'll list only a few here.

- Ephesians 2:10
- 1 Corinthians 1:30
- 2 Corinthians 2:14
- Isaiah 43:4

Chapter 7

Disciplines of Daily Life

Q **How do I keep a happy perspective of my home when I get tired of coming home to the same empty four walls every night or especially when returning from a trip? In other words, how do I keep from resenting my home, the place that is supposed to be a haven and a resting place?**

A It really helps if you have roommates. But if you don't, here are a few suggestions. Be honest with some of your closest friends with whom you can be vulnerable that it can be a little rough always coming home to no one. Let them know that coming home to a message once in a while helps. Don't say this in a way that places expectations on them. Just share your heart. We can keep this in mind for each other, especially for those who live alone. Call now and then, and just leave a simple message saying, "Hi. Was just thinking of you. Hope your day went well." It's a simple thing; it takes half a minute to do, but it can perk up someone's day. It is easier for me to come through the door and see my message light flashing, so I placed my answering machine right by my front door.

Another thing you can do is to place a lot of pictures of those you love all around your house. One year I didn't have anyone with whom to spend the Fourth of July holiday. I sensed the Lord directing me to conquer how I was feeling about that (dejected) by going to the store, buying a whole bunch of picture frames and filling my house with happy pictures of good times with friends and family. What a huge asset this has been. Everywhere I walk in my house, I see reminders all around me of people I love and who love me. Sometimes when I've felt particularly sad or lonely, God has used those photographs to remind me that I'm not always alone, and I won't continue to be alone—it's a passing thing.

In addition, it really helps if you make your home comfortable and appealing. Make it a reflection of who you are, and decorate in such a way that when you have people over, you are proud of your home. Make it warm and inviting. Don't give in to the thinking that because you are the only one who sees it most of the time, it doesn't matter. It's easy to give in to this. But it *does* matter. It makes a difference in the way you feel about yourself. You *are worthy* of a nice home regardless of not having a family who shares it.

I felt God really directed me to take action on this. I sensed Him encouraging me to take this to heart because *He* viewed it as important, because I am important to Him. I'd go over to my married friends' home and see all the ways that their home reflected their family. Sometimes this was hard, because I would contrast it with mine, which had an "emptiness" by comparison. The Lord, however, reminded me that my home was His gift to me. That puts it in a whole new light. I know this might sound trite, but I mean it sincerely. In earnest, if you view your home as God's gift to you, suddenly, it takes on a much higher value than just a place where you live. When this really sunk in to my heart, I began to take a greater interest in my home. I wanted it to reflect Jesus to all who entered. That made all the difference. And to this day, people often tell me that my home is peaceful and calming. Truly that does reflect Jesus.

Another thing that helps keep you feeling that "life" is in your home is to have people over! Make a schedule if you have to in order to stay on track with this objective. Invite people for dinner. Host a barbecue during the summer. Have a Christmas party. Invite your friends' children over. Yes, you can even have the toddlers. You'd be surprised how quickly you can move things around to make your home "childproof." Keep a stash of toys in a closet, and keep some treats around. I have a sand-box and toys in my backyard. Just having them makes me feel good! What a blessing this is to the children, too.

I discuss parameters with parents in advance, and we usu-ally try to determine some harmless things they are allowed to do at my house that they generally are not allowed to do at home. For example, one friend opted to allow her children to actually get *in* the sandbox at my house and get as sandy as they wish! They also are allowed to jump on my bed and have pillow fights (with supervision, of course). As a child, I remember how I loved to visit my grandparents' home! It was fun to go somewhere different that also felt like "home." I enjoyed a sense of belonging there just like at home, and my grandparents always made me feel special. These days, so many children do not live near relatives. It is *wonderful* if we can give them another place that is like "home" where they feel comfortable and special.

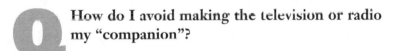

Q **How do I avoid making the television or radio my "companion"?**

A Obviously there is nothing wrong with watching tel-evision or listening to the radio for a *reasonable* amount of time. I bring this up for those who feel compelled to have either the television or radio on *all* the time in order to feel *comfortable*. I'm addressing people who use these devices as a regular substitute for people. While both the television and radio can be entertaining and informative, they are not people. We were made for relationship with *people*! If you allow yourself to rely on the television or radio, you will become less inclined to do the harder thing, which is to pick up the phone and call someone in order to stay "connected."

This practice can subtly steal your motivation to either have people over or to make plans to meet others out. And sometimes God wants to get our attention in solitude.

Constant noise in the background can keep our minds so busy that we don't slow down to "connect" with God and understand what He is trying to convey to us in quietness. The bottom line is that this practice becomes a crutch, and then we become enslaved by it. Instead of having control over when the television and radio are turned on or off, we begin to feel compelled to have one or the other on. I've seen some people become so "addicted" to having background noise that even when friends do come over, they still need to have the television or radio playing in the background. This is bondage!

This practice can be so tempting, especially for those who live alone. The best way to avoid it is not to start in the first place. I have vigorously fought turning to the television or radio as a means of making me "feel" as if someone was there. I keep all of this in proper perspective. These devices have their purpose. They are useful tools. But they are not substitutes for people. Some people *like* to listen to the radio a lot. This is not to say there's something wrong with listening perhaps even a lot. It's the *motive* that counts. Are you listening because you genuinely *enjoy* listening, or are you listening purely to assuage feeling alone?

If you have gotten to the place in your life that you feel you simply must have one or the other turned on, you have to wean yourself off, much like people who are addicted to other things. Like any bondage, it is going to take time and work to get free from it. Pray. Ask God to fill the hole left when you are breaking free. Ask others to pray for you about it. That may be a humbling thing, but God tells us He "gives grace to the humble" (1 Pet. 5:5).

Instead of turning to the television or radio for a sense of people's presence, it is best to get to the place once again where you can be comfortable in the quiet of your home. Turn to God. Many times He draws us to Himself by creating a hunger in us for fellowship. Turn to people as well. Have them over or go out, but don't let electronic devices take their place!

Q How do I break the cycle of filling my schedule with activity just to avoid the pain of being alone? And how do I overcome the problems this creates when I consequently fall behind on life's essential chores?

A Some singles can't stand to be alone or fear how they will feel if they are alone for very long. Sometimes this occurs because they can't face their lives as they are. They may fear that if they have too much time alone, they'll dwell on the negative aspects too much.

Consequently, they may look to people or activities to quell these issues. While it is good to be active and look to people to meet your legitimate relational needs, it's not good if things get out of balance. There is nothing wrong with having a busy schedule. Some people have "type A" personalities. They prefer to be on the go all the time. So let's put aside personality types; that's not the issue. I'm addressing motives again.

You must ask yourself, "Am I filling my schedule to the brim because I don't want to face being alone?" If that's the case, and it is a routine thing, not an occasional thing (because we all do this to some degree), you need to take action. A bondage has formed. It may even look highly spiritual. You may be attending several Bible study groups. You may be active in several ministries of the church. While it's good to serve and not be self-focused, you should have the right motive for serving and not choose to serve merely as a means of distraction.

When people fill their schedules too full, they typically fall behind on life's essential chores. They may burn out and lose their motivation for service and ministry. They also can become worn out. Their work habits may suffer. Their relationships may begin to fray. Time with God diminishes. When this problem is extreme, their health may be jeopardized. Life in general may begin to unravel!

When this happens, what do you do? First, recognize that God could give you gems in the solitude that you are afraid to have. Stop and realize that you are missing out on a lot because you refuse to be still long enough to really commune with God.

Then, get to the root of the problem; do not merely treat the symptoms. Repent for trying to obtain too much satisfaction out of personal relationships at the expense of your relationship with God. Repent of the fears that are driving your decisions to load up your schedule. Repent for not trusting God to help you deal with what you are afraid to face.

Repent not only for the root issues, but also for the fruit of the roots; that is, for whatever fallout has been produced by the roots. For example, repent if you've become neglectful of your personal affairs or if your work or relationships are suffering. Tell God you're sorry, and make it right with whomever you have hurt or offended.

Recognize that it will take time to break bad habits and to deal with the fallout. Be patient. Trust God that as you have brought these issues to Him in prayer, He will change you. He will show you practical ways to change. He will give you the tools and assistance to put new ways of living in place and the courage to face your fears.

Seek out people who are balanced in this area, and ask them how they do it. Proverbs 24:6 states, "For by wise guidance you will wage war, and in abundance of counselors there is victory."

Chapter 8

Realities Concerning Loss and Lack

Q How do I overcome the loss of not having a person in my life who cares about my day-to-day life, no one who just delights in me?

A This is basically the definition of companionship, and it is the chief thing we miss as singles. Implementing the suggestions in chapters fourteen through sixteen is the best way I know to provide for this need. Instead of having one person who is ever by our side, we need to have a variety of folks whose lives are intertwined with ours.

As a practical matter, it is a blessing if God gives you a couple of friends that you tune in with almost daily. But this doesn't happen for everyone, at least not in every phase of our lives. So, an alternative is to try to schedule routine get-togethers with close friends. Perhaps you meet once a week for breakfast. You may schedule dinner once a month with another friend or group of friends. The important thing is to feel the comfort and assurance in your heart that you'll have these get-togethers with friends. They are on the calendar.

That way, in times when you're feeling disconnected, you can take comfort in knowing a gathering is coming. Some people are more spontaneous in nature and don't feel the need to *plan* these get-togethers. So long as they are buoyed up by a sense of connectedness, that's fine. The important thing is having the sheer comfort of knowing there are others in your life from whom you can receive and to whom you can give.

For many of us, this overarching lack truly is the kingpin of pain. If that's the case for you, it is best if you devise a

69

personalized "pain management plan" as touched upon earlier.

Q How do I deal with the fact that I am no one's first (or second or third…) priority?

A This can also be a very hard thing. I have family and some friends who are very high priorities to me, but the best I can hope to be in their pecking order is significantly lower than where they are in mine, because they are married. We have to accept this reality and work within it in as healthy a way as possible. What really matters is that your family and friends love you and are committed to you. When this is the case, it ultimately doesn't matter where you find yourself in the pecking order.

Sure, there will be times when your desire goes unfulfilled because your friend responded to a need that was a higher priority. This happens. When it does, God uses it to crucify your flesh (Gal. 5:24). It is a good opportunity to fulfill Philippians 2:3–4. I regard another as more important than myself, and I look to the interest of others. Regarding someone as "more important" doesn't mean I put myself "lower" than others in an unhealthy way. That is demeaning. It means that I follow the example Jesus set—He was a servant, which is totally amazing, since He is God.

I don't stop there, though. I also bring my desire to God. I ask Him to fill it another way. If He does, great. If He doesn't, I accept that.

We can be consoled by remembering that we are a priority to God. I take comfort in that. But I don't think God faults us for feeling what we feel in human terms. Couples know that there is another person to whom they are the absolute first priority. (They may not always feel as though they are, when work, for example, gets in the way. But in reality, the fact of their marriage makes them first, period.) There is a real comfort in that—one they may be so accustomed to that they don't even realize the comfort they derive from it. God knows that is missing for singles. It's OK to feel what we feel about it. It's just that we can't let it take us down "pity" lane. It's a fact about being single that we must accept and to which we must adjust.

Q **How do I deal with feeling that no one would notice if I suddenly fell off the face of the earth?**

A Unless you truly are a recluse, the feeling described above is just that—a *feeling*. It is not the truth. People would notice. And people would mourn. Nonetheless, feelings are important. We shouldn't simply shrug them off, as if they're nothing. I deal with my feelings in several ways.

First, I recognize it is a feeling, not a fact. Of itself, that is somewhat comforting.

Second, because it is a feeling, I remind myself that it will pass. Facts hang around, and they have to be dealt with in a more concrete way. But feelings come and go. So, I console myself by *consciously* telling myself that I'm not going to *continue* feeling this way. All the while, I'm praying, telling God how I feel, and gaining an assurance that how I feel matters to Him.

Somewhere in this process, I also reflect upon the truth. I think about the people who would notice. As I go through these processes, I am training myself each time to deal better and better with my emotions. I don't negate them, because God does not. He made us with emotions, and they are a great asset to us. He beckons us to come to Him with our emotions. So I do. He helps me sort truth from lies.

Ultimately, He leads me to the truths that are most important for the situation I am in. It is critical to realize that God wants us to work through this *with* Him. He does not despise the emotions that can cause us to get off track. As God walks me through all the things I'm feeling—and the things I'm thinking because of what I'm feeling, He shows me how Satan has lied to me. This is the discernment process, and each time we go through it, we get better and better at discerning truth from lies.

Q **How do I deal with having no milestones to which to look forward—major wedding anniversaries, children going to college, graduating, marrying, having grandchildren?**

A First of all, if you have good, solid, family-based friendships (which we will discuss in Part II), you can genuinely enter into the joy of anticipating special events in the lives of your friends' children. When you deeply love them, this is a true joy.

Second, *look* for things in your life to celebrate. There are things, but in our culture, we tend to overlook them. We can start some new trends. We have to pioneer this, but I trust it will be worth it for those who come behind us. For example, to me, writing this book was an accomplishment, so I had a big celebration. Have you always dreamed of having a big celebration like a wedding? Well, save up some money and throw the party of your dreams. You don't have to have a specific reason—desiring to gather the people you love in one big festive event is reason enough. You can even hire a photographer and videographer so you'll have great pictures and captured memories for years to come. Be creative. Think outside the box. Lead the way for others.

Q **How do I deal with fears of what will happen to me when I am old and with wondering who will take care of me?**

A God reminds us in Matthew 6:25–34 that He takes care of the birds of the air and the flowers of the field—He will take care of us! Philippians 4:6–7 reads, "Be anxious for nothing, but in everything by prayer and supplication with thanksgiving let your requests be made known to God. And the peace of God, which surpasses all comprehension, shall guard your hearts and your minds in Christ Jesus."

These are great passages to help us conquer general anxiety, and there also are scriptures that address our specific fears about old age.

> Listen to Me, O house of Jacob,
> And all the remnant of the house of Israel,
> You who have been borne by Me from birth,
> And have been carried from the womb;
> Even to your old age, I shall be the same,
> And even to your graying years I shall bear you!
>
> —ISAIAH 46:3–4

(Because these verses are a prophecy to Israel, we cannot make them a promise specifically for us, yet they show God's heart and faithfulness toward His people.)

> I have been young, and now I am old;
> Yet I have not seen the righteous forsaken,
> Or his descendants begging bread.
>
> —PSALM 37:25

> For such is God,
> Our God forever and ever;
> He will guide us until death.
>
> —PSALM 48:14

It is important to *exercise faith* and *believe* God will provide for you. Instead of passively hoping that God will take care of you, this is one of those areas where you may be required to *actively* assert your faith that God will take care of you, even if you have no spouse or dependents upon whom to rely.

We can strive to emulate Joshua and Caleb. They were faithful to God and *actively* asserted their faith in His word when they accompanied the other ten spies into the Promised

Land. (See Numbers 13.) The remaining ten did not stand in faith. In the end, who entered the Promised Land? It was Joshua and Caleb—the two who actively believed. And Caleb gave this testimony as he was rewarded with his parcel of land:

> I am eighty-five years old today. I am still as strong today as I was in the day Moses sent me [he was forty when Moses sent him as a spy]; as my strength was then, so my strength is now, for war and for going out and coming in.
>
> —JOSHUA 14:10–11

We can be encouraged when we think of what God did in the old age of two other specific biblical characters. Elijah was taken up to heaven in a whirlwind (2 Kings 2:11). (And you can't say to yourself, "Well, that was *Elijah*, and I'm just *me*," because in James 5:17, we see that "Elijah was a man *with a nature like ours...*") As for Moses, the Bible says that "although Moses was one hundred and twenty years old when he died, his eye was not dim, nor his vigor abated" (Deut. 34:7). God Himself buried Moses. We see in these lives that God provided for His servants. He may not take us up in a whirlwind; He might not bury us Himself; but He *will* see to it that we are taken care of.

Q In the past, I've been hurt when single friends have started dating someone new and left me behind. How do I overcome the resistance I now feel to making new friends, fearing the cycle will keep repeating itself?

A This is a self-protection issue. We've been hurt in the past and want to shield ourselves from similar future wounds. The major issue here is that we don't know if a person to whom we feel newly drawn in friendship may be faithful or unfaithful; only God knows. In *every* relationship, we do not know what lies down the road.

That is where trust in God comes in.

His Word is a lamp to our feet and a light to our path (Ps. 119:105). Usually a lamp covers only a small distance. Even today's high-powered flashlights can project light only so far. I believe God illustrates in this passage that we are on a faith walk with Him. He shows us as much of the path as we need to see. We walk the path of every relationship *with* God. We are to "watch over [our] heart" (Prov. 4:23). This means to use wisdom in your choices; it does not mean to "lock your heart" so that no one may get in.

Even in the very best of relationships—and sometimes *especially* in the very best of relationships—we'll be hurt. But we can't let that stop us from entering into relationships. On this side of heaven, we all sin. Not only do others hurt us, but also we hurt others. We hope and pray others will forgive us when we fail. We should be willing to extend forgiveness to others when they hurt us. We do not want to be like the slave who was forgiven his entire huge debt by the king, yet refused to forgive a small debt by a fellow slave. (See Matthew 18:21–35.)

Being hurt by people can produce one of two contrasted things in us. Either we can let the wounds inflicted by others cause us slowly but surely to wall ourselves off from people out of self-protection, or we can recognize the power of God to heal us and even make us better people through the wounds inflicted by others. When you wall yourself off, you are sure to lose a lot. When you stay open, though the risk is real, still, you will gain much in the long run.

Q **I keep hoping I'll meet my future spouse soon, so I hold off making big decisions that could be seriously impacted if I become engaged. How long do I wait to make significant decisions like these?**

A We would greatly benefit from teaching that touches on some of the more practical aspects of life that are still tied to theological concepts. We need to develop balanced approaches in a number of areas. One area involves the balance between putting life "on hold" as we are waiting and hoping for a spouse, and moving ahead with major decisions despite the uncertainty of our future.[1] I call this the "waiting game."

For example, I was uncertain about how long to wait to buy a house, knowing that if I found the man of my dreams and had to sell it too soon, I could suffer quite a financial loss. Some are uncertain how long to postpone making significant decisions concerning career paths, mission fields or relocating. At some point, though, you just have to move forward with those kinds of decisions, accepting the fact that there are risks no matter the path. Potential financial losses or other possible losses can pale in comparison to what is lost if we place life on hold for too long.

When faced with these types of "how long?" questions, here are three things I suggest you do. First, pray for guidance and then earnestly *watch* for it. Second, seek wise counsel from others whom you respect and admire. If possible, choose people who have successfully maneuvered through a decision similar to the one you face. Third, do your homework—that is, study your options. Be diligent to weigh important factors. Trust God, and He will likely use all these avenues to show you what to do.

Chapter 9

A Deeper Look at Well-Intentioned Advice

Q Why do I feel like there's a piece of the puzzle I can't quite seem to put my finger on when married people tell me not to place too much emphasis on how fulfilled I will be by a spouse?

A Some couples respond to us by exhorting us not to place too much stock in how fulfilled we will be by a spouse. The implication is that we are looking too much to a person to bring satisfaction. Even with our God-given need for companionship, I wholeheartedly agree that singles should be cautioned against placing too much emphasis on finding satisfaction or fulfillment in a spouse. But there is another component to this whole issue that many people miss.

For many of us, it is not that we place too much emphasis on the joy a spouse will bring; it is facing the reality of the loss of all the other things in life that having a spouse often allows. I call this the longing for marriage *and its accoutrements*. I'm talking about accoutrements like having children and grandchildren, looking forward to and celebrating major life milestones, having the comfort of knowing you have family to care for you in your old age, taking family vacations and having a wider social and family circle.

Basically, I'm referring to the enjoyment of so many of the normal things married folks experience in life—like sex—and not just sex, but simple affection. For example, couples may take for granted a kiss hello and good-bye. But we may not enjoy a kiss, have a hand to hold, or have an arm around us when we sit in church. And this may be not just for a week or

a month, but possibly for years on end. We miss having someone excitedly waiting for us at the airport or having someone
who wants to be by our side in the hospital. Singles with no
children also miss things like cheering at our child's Little
League baseball games, clapping at their recitals and tearing
up at their graduations and weddings.

This is not to overglamorize these things. Family life is not
perfect because life's not perfect. Marriage is hard work. Raising
children is hard work, especially in today's culture. Sin has
marred everything, and relating to a spouse and to children
always carries unique challenges. Hard things happen in life to
the married as well as to the single. Despite all of this, we do
need to acknowledge that there are a whole lot of things that
families naturally experience in life that singles don't. When
you pile them all together, it can easily feel like a mountain of
loss to a single.

I don't want to emphasize the negatives here, but I state these
things because we need to recognize that it truly is not just the
lack of a spouse that many of us mourn. It is the lack of what
many feel is just normal life, coupled with the ever-present
question of whether we ever will experience these things.

So when your married friends exhort you not to place too
much importance on a spouse, lovingly and tactfully help them
understand these additional components of the whole picture
that they may not see or understand. Recognize that it is normal for you to want family and friends to understand and validate the legitimacy of your unfulfilled longings. Most likely,
the more they understand, the more they will not only validate
you, but will respond compassionately. However, whether they
understand or not, it's important that you recognize these
things yourself. Only then can you move past this to a point of
living successfully despite these unfulfilled longings.

 **Why do some pieces of advice leave me feeling
guilty or angry or empty?**

A There is a lack of understanding about certain truths as they apply specifically to singles, such as the universal human need for companionship, the significance of accoutrements that accompany marriage and the need for balancing desire and contentment. It is thus common for singles to hear well-intentioned yet unhelpful comments such as: "Just go to Jesus and deepen your relationship with Him." "Serve others more to get your mind off of yourself." "God just wants you all to Himself." "You need to learn to be content." "Well, at least you can go to the bathroom alone; my children don't even let me have that time alone! I'd trade you any day!"

While there is truth imbedded in many of these types of comments, the reason they often are unhelpful despite the associated truths is because they are not appropriately balanced with other truths that make the whole picture more genuine and more reflective of God's heart for us. A key ingredient missing from these types of comments is validation of the legitimate needs and longings of singles. For example, being told to "just go to Jesus" oversimplifies the complexity of our God-given need for human companionship. Jokingly contrasting the desire to have alone time in the bathroom trivializes the genuineness of our earnest and heartfelt battle against loneliness. We do not say things in jest to couples who cannot conceive or when a spouse dies. The relational hole we live with can cause as much anguish as the inability to have children (which many of us also face for different reasons) or losing a spouse. Our challenges call for similar sensitivity coupled with wise and balanced counsel.

When advice isn't balanced, it can create internal conflict. For example, when people would tell me that God was not allowing me to marry because He wanted me "all to Himself," I had a hard time not relating to God as if He were the "Beast" in *Beauty and the Beast*. In my heart I knew that God is good and loving, and certainly not selfish. But I'd find myself in conflict. If God wanted me all to Himself, on the one hand, that made me feel "special"—kind of like the princess. On the other hand, I was holed up in the castle just because He wanted me to be alone with Him. I'd think, *Well, He's God; He has that right.* So I'd try to yield myself willingly. But I'd go back and forth between seeing God as He really is and seeing Him as the "Beast." That was awful.

The better you understand, in a balanced and healthy way, the legitimacy of many of the things you feel and the right perspective of how God views them, the better you will handle the well-intentioned advice given to you. Instead of such advice dampening your spirit or sending you in the wrong direction, you can remain at peace in your heart, knowing the truth as it applies to you. Hopefully, you also will be able gently, lovingly and patiently to help others learn better ways of responding to singles who open up their hearts and express what's in them. You can help others see that they can respond to the grief or longing expressed by singles with compassion and empathy, stating that they recognize the hardships and understand the need for companionship. After affirming that, they can follow through with hope-filled, faith-filled positive comments (said sincerely so as not to seem like trite remarks). They can remind singles that God does have a plan for our lives and that even though life may be painful now, it won't always be. They can tell us they are standing with us, trusting God to meet our genuine needs for relational fulfillment. They can affirm that God truly may have a mate waiting in the wings. They can remind us that it only takes *one!* Courageously and humbly seize the opportunity when God opens the door for you to explain lovingly the benefit of these types of encouraging statements in contrast to comments that can actually be demeaning. Doing so is good not only for you and the one to whom you are speaking, but ultimately also for the whole body of Christ.

Q Why is it generally not helpful for someone to try to console or encourage you in your singleness by telling you to be glad you are not in a hard or failing marriage?

A Many times people have tried to console me by telling me to be happy I am not in a bad marriage. Or some have told me not to dream of having a wonderful American family. They counsel me instead to let my mind dwell on the fact that not all marriages are great, and not all situations are so idyllic. People have often said something like, "Well, it really is better to be single than to be married to the wrong person," and "You know, marriage can be *really* hard." I've also been reminded of the high divorce rate. But this type of counsel doesn't work. It backfires despite people's good intentions.

I strongly believe we need to be balanced and not look at family life in an unrealistic, hyper-idealized way. Thus, gentle reminders like those above *every now and then* can be helpful. However, for many of us, these types of negatively focused comments come too frequently for too long. Problems emerge when, over the years, our focus is continually directed toward negative images as a means of helping us, as a means of counterbalancing our normal, healthy desires.

These types of comments cause problems for several reasons. First, some of these comments come across as if we are left with only two unappealing choices in life—better to be *single* than married to the *wrong* person. Second, they assume the worst: "You might marry the wrong person." Yes, but I might marry the right one! A simple analogy is that this is like telling someone who loves oranges not to go to the store and buy any because he or she might pick out a bad one. Third, it's as if they assume our desires spring from a very rationally based decision-making process.

Most people would never think of telling a couple who

can't conceive, "Well, if you had a child, he or she might have a defect or grow up to have major problems." Nor would we say, "Well, you know, raising children is *really* hard," as if these kinds of comments would actually be useful and effective in trying to talk the couple out of their desire. We don't say those kinds of things because we know intuitively that reason and logic don't motivate a couple's desire for children. Their decision isn't calculated like a math problem on the basis of statistics that tell them their chances of success! They are willing to take risks because it is *worth* it to them! The same is true regarding the desire to marry. So if you've wondered why this type of advice just hasn't seemed quite right, hopefully now you recognize why.

It would be one thing if this type of advice simply fell flat and didn't really help us, but it doesn't stop there. This type of advice can actually hurt us and ultimately hurt the whole body of Christ. Here's what happens. When we hear these types of comments over and over, we can begin to think that the way to handle our desire to marry is by countering it with bleak pictures—negative pictures of the life we think we would like to live but can't. Some develop a "sour grapes" theory of marriage—"I want to have this thing, but I can't, so instead I'm going to convince myself of how rotten it is anyway."

We know it's a mistake to think that way, but why? Well, Philippians 4:8 gives the answer:

> Whatever is true, whatever is honorable, whatever is right, whatever is pure, whatever is lovely, whatever is of good repute, if there is any excellence and if anything worthy of praise, *let your mind dwell on these things.*
>
> —EMPHASIS ADDED

We are to dwell on these *good* things. It doesn't say "look on the bleak side" or "always consider the cup half empty." It is interesting when you think about it—we tell singles to look on the bright side of being single by looking on the dark side of marriage. Instead, let's tell them to look on the bright side of both!

If we paint this bleak, ugly picture of marriage in an attempt to quell our desires, it can spill over and color the way we view our friends' marriages, the marriages of our pastors and other leaders, our siblings' marriages and others. It just grows. Eventually it will leave us fearful to be married if and when an actual marriage prospect comes along. How horrible! How tragically unnecessary! We are much better off by purposefully dwelling on the strong and healthy marriages we know. It is even better, far better, if we also conscientiously pray for the marriages of all those we know!

Now you are armed with discernment. When you hear comments like those mentioned above, keep the right perspective. Don't let the negativity get down into your bones. Vigorously resist looking at the holy institution of marriage in a negative light and looking at your own future potential in marriage negatively. We all, single and married, have a God-given responsibility to support this sacred institution for our own good, for the good of the church and for the good of society. Let us do so in the fear of God.

Chapter 10

Holidays, Vacations and Other Events

Q **How do I deal with receiving Christmas cards, year after year, with family photos and everyone's update on their children?**

A We all experience this, don't we? Year after year we receive Christmas cards, letters and photos updating us on the lives of our friends, many of who now are married. Each year you get updated on the vast array of changes taking place in the lives of your married friends. Meanwhile, you might feel that your life hasn't changed much at all. It may seem barren in stark contrast, especially against a sea of cards.

The holidays are hard enough to deal with, let alone adding this component. During some of those years when I wasn't handling things well, a part of my fleshly nature wanted to toss them all in the trash. I certainly did not want to "display" them and have them all staring me in the face day after day. The devil used to use these as such powerful weapons in his arsenal against me. But in Isaiah 54:17, the Bible says, "No weapon that is formed against you shall prosper." So, how do we get a grip on this?

I was honest with God. I told God how I was feeling and poured out my heart to Him. I asked Him to bear my pain when receiving a new card was painful or difficult. Not all days were hard, but on days that were, I needed to be honest and pour it out on Him. He wants to bear our burdens, take our pain and comfort us.

I told the Lord, "It's not that I don't wish happiness for them; You know I do. You know I'm so happy that they get to experience this. It's just that You know how much I want this, too—and it hurts." At times I'd also add, "And Lord, another year, yet another holiday without a family. How long, Lord? Will it be forever? And if it is, can I bear it? O God, please help me. Please comfort me."

Then I'd wait for God to respond. I didn't just pray this to the air and walk away. I asked these things believing God would respond. Sometimes He's responded immediately, but when not, I've asked Him to help my eyes and heart to see His response when it came. Then I thanked Him.

This process is such a relationship builder. Instead of shunning God in my anger and despair, I go through the experience *with* Him. Just as sharing this kind of heartfelt pain with a friend builds and strengthens the friendship, so it does our relationship with God, if we let it. And I believe this is exactly what He wants. He didn't specifically design this painful spot for us *so that* we would deepen our relationship with Him. But relating to Him like this is our "avenue of escape"—the fulfillment of His promise that He'd never allow us to be tempted beyond what we are able, and with the temptation, He would always provide a means of escape (1 Cor. 10:13).

After pouring my heart out, I could usually enter into what those stories and pictures were all about—the outworking of God's plan in the lives of my friends and their families. God demonstrates His grace and glorifies Himself through their lives. Instead of allowing those pictures to be used by the devil to remind me of what I did not have, I would turn my attention to Jesus and worship Him for His goodness displayed through those lives. God, in His goodness, would then strengthen my faith for what He has in store for me. He would remind me of Jeremiah 29:11:

> "For I know the plans I have for you," declares the
> LORD, "plans to prosper you and not to harm you,

plans to give you hope and a future."

—NIV

When I thought about God's purposes for my life, I did not fall prey to the notion that my life is insignificant in contrast. I chose to believe that God is glorifying Himself through my life as well.

As this process continued, God brought me to the place where I now use these Christmas cards as an opportunity to pray for these friends and their families. This can become an awesome tradition between you and God. God also brought me to the place where I do, in fact, love to display these cards.

I have another practical suggestion for times when you struggle with this. Sometimes we get swamped with a lot of cards all at once. But maybe you feel your heart can handle reading only one or two a day. Then do that. Set a limit and don't feel guilty about it. Store them up, and even if you don't read some of them until after Christmas, that's OK. By taking this action, you are being a good steward of your heart, not demanding more of it than you can take at the time.

Q **Another holiday is coming. How do I deal with not having special plans, having nowhere to go and the feelings created by always having to fit in with plans made by a family when I do not have any input in creating those plans?**

A When a holiday approaches, I make it a point to be prepared in a practical way. First I think outside the box and consider what would be an appealing celebration for me. I try not to give in automatically to thinking about all the reasons why a fresh idea I have can't work. In other words, I try to be positive. (As an aside, it is so easy to conclude automatically that others will be busy or will not want to do what we'd like to do. I think this is a tactic the devil uses to keep the family of God from coming together. Have you had people tell you, "You know, I was going to call you, but I didn't because I assumed you were probably busy"? I know I've let this thinking get in my way countless times. If *I* think that, and *others* think that, chances are good that this sort of thing happens all the time. It's even easier to give into this way of thinking over the holidays. Resist it!)

Pray and ask God for direction. He may lead you to do something you don't exactly want to do. Or He may give you a fabulous idea that takes you by surprise. Whatever the case may be, trust Him. If He leads me to do something about which I'm not thrilled, I try to step out in faith, remembering in the back of my mind that His plan is the best.

Some of us may be close to a friend's family and hope and pray that God will move upon their hearts to invite us over. There is nothing wrong with asking God to do that. But if it does not happen, I suggest *you* come up with an idea— something you'd like to invite that family to do—and then ask. It may be tough to ask. You may have to fight off much insecurity. Do it anyway. Ask God for help to rise above your fears of feeling silly and being rejected. As I have developed the courage to express my viewpoint and desires in a tactful way and in a way that does not impose demands upon the other people involved, I have found that my family and friends are very willing to accommodate my needs and desires. Most of the time, they just truly have not understood how I felt.

I like to focus on meeting the need of someone else who may be struggling over a holiday, such as on Mother's Day. I ask myself if there's a single mom I can bless, or perhaps someone who had a miscarriage.

I think the two most important factors in successfully dealing with holidays are:

- Pray and ask God what He wants for you; then obey as best you know how, to the degree you sense direction from God.

- Be realistic about your desires, what you have to
  give and what you need. Then try to design a
  workable plan that takes this assessment into
  account.

Don't be self-centered and self-serving, but don't be in self-denial, either. Don't be stoic and ignore holidays altogether. You *can* have joy by entering in. Believe that and act on it.

Q **Another summer is coming…how do I deal with lack of vacation plans…no one with whom to vacation? How do I cope with hearing my married friends talk about their wonderful family vacation plans year after year without becoming bitter and resentful?**

A This answer is similar to the one above regarding holidays. I try to think of what I'd like to do. Then, with a positive outlook, I try to find a person or people who'd like to do the same thing—both single and married. I've had years when I could not find anyone to vacation with, so I took the time off and spent it productively around my house mixed with doing fun things with friends locally in a more relaxed and leisurely way than I can when I'm under my normal schedule. These types of "vacations" have been a great use of that time off from work. I feel a sense of accomplishment and also reap the benefits of being better connected with local friends.

What you may have to fight is doing something just for the sake of doing *something*. That devalues us. There have been times when I've done this, driven either by loneliness or low self-worth. I learned the hard way—don't do it! These experiences left me depressed either about wasted time, wasted money or because of feeling that I demeaned myself out of desperation.

I try to head into the summer with some sort of plan for how I am going to vacation, or at least special things I plan to do to make the summer fun. This helps counter the feelings that surface when married friends begin talking about their family vacations. It seems like the devil always tries to put in our face what we're missing out on. I know I must actively counter that. If I sit around passively, making no plans for myself, it is so much easier to cave in to self-pity.

One way to "resist the devil" is to take action. I make a plan. I head into the summer both offensively and defensively. I have something to look forward to, and I decide in advance that I will be thankful about those plans so that when others share their plans with me, I do not feel left out of life. Of course, even if I don't have any fun plans at all, God still requires me to rejoice with my friends who do. We must passionately resist becoming envious, bitter and resentful. These are wretched enemies—far worse to grapple with than a summer of no plans! Don't walk with them for a day or even a minute! Ask God for the grace to resist all temptations to enter into these traps.

Q **How do I handle bridal and baby showers? Weddings?**

A I keep two major things in mind when attending showers and weddings. First, I want to be a blessing to the people involved. Second, God has His plans for me, and I trust Him.

When I attend these events, temptations abound for me to begin looking at my life and feeling sad. Forewarned is forearmed. It's wise for me to go "prayed up." That is, I know it is good to make a concerted effort to pray earnestly beforehand, allowing God to shore me up. Not only is my fleshly nature going to want to send me down the wrong path, but the devil will, too. These events are ripe occasions for the devil to whisper all kinds of damaging things in your ear. So it just makes sense to prepare yourself as best as you can beforehand.

When I'm there at the event, I try to focus my attention on the person or people in the spotlight. I ask myself, "How can I bless them? How can I encourage them? How can I demonstrate tangibly that I am happy for them and wish them all the best?" With these types of questions as my focus, it becomes harder for my mind to start wandering off thinking about my own lack.

Even so, it usually does wander sooner or later in that direction. But again, because I prepare myself in advance, I'm ready. For one, I know what those negative thoughts are going to sound like, so I'm more tuned in to recognize them when they come. Here's a sampling of the negative thoughts for which you should always be on the lookout:

- "Look how happy she is…when will it ever be *my* turn? *Will* it ever be my turn?"

- "Here I am, giving of myself at *another* shower."

- "Does anybody here even recognize that this might be a little hard for me?"

- "I can't believe this; she's *half* my age, and she's getting married!"

- "Oh gee, now I have to sit here and listen to all these wives and mothers give advice from their years of experience."

I dislike admitting that these kinds of things go through my mind. I wish it weren't true, but these are the kinds of things we have to battle.

God has a solution, though, as always. We read in 2 Corinthians 10:4–5:

> For the weapons of our warfare are not of the flesh, but divinely powerful for the destruction of fortresses. We are destroying speculations and every lofty thing raised up against the knowledge of God, and we are *taking every thought captive* to the obedience of Christ.
>
> —EMPHASIS ADDED

Your key is in this verse. You must take those negative thoughts captive. They hurt you, they can hurt others, and they do not glorify God. A wonderful pastor gave me a great picture of what it's like to take our thoughts captive (thank you, David Houston). Picture your hand reaching into your head, grabbing that thought, pulling it out and casting it down. It has no power over you; you have caged it and hurled it down. You have to be ruthless in your approach to these types of negative thoughts. Don't entertain them. You can't afford to give in to what, at the moment, seems like the luxury of letting it roll around a few times before you take it captive. As soon as you recognize you're thinking those types of thoughts, take action immediately. If you don't, then one thought leads to another, and then another. Before you know it, you will be depressed and self-focused. That hinders you from being a blessing to others because your eyes are on yourself instead of on God and on your friends.

That is the defensive mode. The offensive mode is to remind yourself, when thoughts like that try to take over, that God has His own unique plan for you. Actively place your trust in His character and His goodness and in the fact that His plan is a good one. Even if you don't particularly *like* God's plan for you, take comfort in thinking about Him, who He is—not about His *plan*. When you focus on His goodness, then the part of the plan you dislike won't seem so important. At some point, either here or in heaven, His plan and how you fit into it will all make sense. So while you walk the part of His plan that you dislike, the thing that keeps you going will be trusting in Him and His faithfulness. Consequently, work to replace the negative thoughts with centered and anchored thoughts about God and His nature.

One last point on this topic—sometimes, quite a few showers and weddings can occur in rapid succession. Those times can be tough. It can feel as if you are in a boxing ring, and you keep getting hit. Maybe you succumb at some point. Don't beat yourself up over it (Rom. 8:1–2). Just get up, repent and keep walking. Proverbs 24:16 says, "A righteous man falls seven times, and rises again..." Another good strategy for times like this is simply to treat yourself. Let yourself do something special—something in which you would not normally indulge. In reasonable measure, I think this is a healthy strategy.

Q **How do I handle going to a formal event (office holiday party, fund-raising dinner, wedding)? Do I just not go? Do I find someone to escort me even though I have no interest in the person? And if I do take someone, how do I cope with all the rumors afterward? How do I handle it if I decide to just go alone?**

A I know there are some singles who will not attend a formal event unless they can be accompanied by someone. I am not one of them. Perhaps this is because I'm such a "people person." I want to be where the action is. If it's an event I personally would *like* to attend, I don't let the lack of an escort get in my way. Oh, trust me, I know how awkward it feels to walk into a big ballroom-type facility alone. I know how it feels to take your place at a table for eight with three couples, and "Oh my, there's this empty seat" so obviously screaming to everyone, "She's alone!" I mean, you're already fighting the thoughts that people are looking at you through the stereotypical image of singles. Now, you have this chair next to you that is continuously reminding everyone that you're by yourself. You think to yourself, *Oh no; look how obvious it is. There's no way to hide it! I'm doomed.* I say this half jokingly because really, mostly, I get over all of that pretty quickly. There's the initial "plunge into cold water" feeling, and then it's over. After that, I just focus on people and enjoy their company.

The pangs that actually are worse for me are the ones I feel both getting ready and coming home alone. While I'm getting ready, it's easy to think, *I wish I were getting ready for someone special.* And although I'm motivated to look my best anyway, there is a part of me that thinks, *Why bother?* I want to hope that perhaps I'll meet someone special there. But then I think of all the previous events I've attended where that didn't happen, and I just think, *Oh, well. It's important to look my best anyway, even though it doesn't seem to matter.* Coming home, I have to wrestle with, *OK, another formal down, and I'm still driving home and walking through my front door alone.*

So, how do you deal with all of this? Sometimes people give an answer that I think can sound trite. They say, "Picture Jesus as your date."

Here's my answer: Jesus goes with me. Jesus is my Savior. He lives in my heart. He goes *everywhere* with me—to work, to the grocery store, to the restaurant, to the formal and home through my front door alone. I tell Him how I feel. I ask for His grace when it's a hard drive home. Sometimes I've cried after I've gotten home. He's with me as I cry, and He knows exactly how I feel and why I feel it. And He cares. He promises to comfort me, and when I let Him, He does. Many times I do just fine and enjoy myself from start to finish. But for reasons I don't always understand, sometimes I don't. And that's OK. The reality is, sometimes it just is going to hurt. But He is there.

Here's how I approach the escort issue. If I have a friend I can ask to escort me, I make my intentions clear from the beginning. By so doing, I don't in any way lead a man to make something more out of the invitation than simply a friend escorting a friend. This way, we both are clear, and no one is left wondering what the other is thinking. As for possible rumors afterwards, "Oh, well." People are going to think what they are going to think. My friends will know the real story. Others can ask me for clarification. If they don't, and I find myself in a conversation where it's simple to interject a clarification, then I do. Beyond that there's nothing I can do about it. I let it go.

CONCLUSION TO PART I

Currently, there is a little baton passing among us. We can turn this around by encouraging those who are down the road further to give "road maps," so to speak, to those coming behind them. This, coupled with solid teaching from pastors, will help us escape some avoidable pain. The energy we use to reinvent the wheel—that is, to figure out how to overcome these common challenges on our own—we can instead give to moving forward in ministry and other godly pursuits.

I sometimes mourn the loss of all the time and energy I spent grappling with these issues. I believe I could have been more effective in the kingdom of God had I received solid teaching to help me walk through these quagmires *as a single*. I believe Jesus feels the same compassion for many singles today as when He observed the multitudes in Israel. Matthew 9:36 says that He felt compassion "because their problems were so great and they didn't know where to go for help. They were like sheep without a shepherd" (NLT). Right after this statement in Matthew, we find the account of Jesus commissioning the twelve disciples. And after this statement in Mark, Jesus had the twelve disciples feed the five thousand (Mark 6:34–44). Is He commissioning you to be a shepherd who will lead and feed other singles? The harvest is plentiful. The workers are few (Matt. 9:37). Be a worker!

PART II

TOGETHER IN GOD'S FAMILY

You may not have your own family just yet, but Jesus has given you another family—the church. Just as no family is perfect, neither is the church. Until now, the church may not have felt like a family to you. But imperfections do not stop us from striving toward the ideal. We still want to work toward having healthy families and churches. That's what Part II is about—how to push past the imperfections and become the family God intends us to be to one another in the church.

To do this, we first need to understand how we got where we are now and the weaknesses in our current church culture that prevent us from operating more as a family. Then we can look at how to do our part to remove obstacles and to build relationships. I pray you will catch the vision God has for His bride to be beautifully woven together as one family.

Chapter 11

It's Not Good for Man (or Woman) to Be Alone

One of the primary things you need to understand about yourself, especially as it relates to our goal of making the church a family, is that you have *legitimate* relational needs. We *all* do. I make this point strongly because for various reasons (partially touched upon in Part I), you may struggle in many ways to know whether it's OK to have relational needs.

Many singles work hard to convince themselves and the world that it's just fine to be single and that they understand marriage doesn't "solve our problems." But in doing so, we seem to have gone too far. We seem to have come to the point where we can't acknowledge that we need...and rightly desire...to be in relationship with others. Knowing that marriage isn't the answer is great, but we need the pendulum to swing back in the opposite direction to gain balance; to recognize again the very real truth that we do, in fact, have relational needs!

Let's settle the question by looking at the biblical basis for our relational needs. The very first "problem" God addressed in the Bible was the fact that "it is not good for the man to be *alone*" (Gen. 2:18, emphasis added). Adam enjoyed unbroken fellowship with God, a perfect fellowship not yet marred by sin, and a totally satisfying paradise. Yet, it wasn't good for him to be without others. This is the first thing God described as "not good" in all His Creation up to that point, which highlights an important truth: No matter the depth and sweetness of your fellowship with God, you need relationship with *others* as well as with God.

God Himself made you that way. You are made in His

image. He is a relational God, aptly depicted in that He exists
in a Trinity and paid the highest possible price to establish a
relationship with you. So don't despise or feel guilty about
your relational needs. They are God given.

Companionship and belonging are our two chief relational
needs. Having companionship means having at least one person with whom you feel safe and comfortable, at least one
with whom you can be yourself and be confident you are
loved. It's enjoying the sense of having a person walking
beside you comfortably whether in silence or conversation—
one who cares about the details of your life.

Having a sense of belonging means you feel connected in a
meaningful way to others who are important to you. You're
part of a group. You share common goals and values. You trust
one another. You can accomplish certain things in a corporate
sense. This makes you feel stronger than you do merely on
your own.

While these needs can be met in a variety of ways, most of
us desire that they be primarily met through our own family.
For you, this natural desire is unfulfilled in varying degrees,
depending on your circumstances. You may have no children,
or have children but no spouse, and you may not live near any
siblings or parents. If your relational needs are to be satisfied,
you must look to other sources. Unfortunately, in today's culture, you come up against barriers that make it hard to satisfy
these needs even by other means.

If that is true for you, that brings us right back to, "It's not
good for man to be alone." If your relational needs are not
being adequately met, this causes problems. Just as we physically decay and eventually die if our physical needs are not
met adequately, our emotional, psychological and spiritual
selves are harmed when our relational needs are unmet. Be
assured that *God* knows this is a problem, and He wants to
correct it. Others may try to minimize your unmet relational
needs, but God never will. You must believe in your heart

that God wants to solve this problem for you. Once you believe He wants to solve it, you can work with Him to search out His resources and answers for you.

For years I was stuck trying to be content with a meager portion of relationships in my life that were dwindling ever more as each friend got married. I thought I was supposed to learn to accept increasing amounts of isolation. I thought God had chosen this for me, so I needed to submit myself willingly to this lifestyle and learn how to love what apparently God loved about having me in it. I labored under a sense of condemnation because I could not consistently maintain the upper hand on how I felt about being single. Many people with loving intentions counseled me that if I would deepen my relationship with Jesus, and if I would discipline my mind, I would remain victorious. People who know me know I maintain a strong and vibrant relationship with God and that I discipline my thought life. Despite these strengths, I was not always able to live above the aches caused by singleness.

Eventually, God relieved me by allowing me to see that singles in modern American culture are living outside of His intended design. He never intended us to live such isolated lives. When we are not living in accordance with His design, we will experience the negative effects.

THE NEED FOR CULTURAL CHANGE

You may have felt for a long time that the onus for your relational aches rested entirely on you, that there was something wrong with you that you needed to discern and correct. But God is revealing that the elements for victory over the challenges you face go beyond controlling your thoughts and developing your relationship with Him.

Yes, those are vital elements, but the degree of success you are able to achieve results from and depends upon the culture in which you live. Until certain aspects of our culture—especially our church culture—change, we will continue to gain and maintain only partial success in overcoming the aches arising from unmet relational needs.

Some people suggest that everything can be overcome by attitude adjustment. A good attitude is critical in life, but it doesn't resolve all challenges, and God never intended that it should. Our surroundings *do* affect us. Sociologists readily confirm this.

Expecting that singles should merely adopt a better attitude about being single is an unbalanced approach. Now that I understand the role culture plays, I have a different perspective when people tell singles simply to "be content." It's similar to the problem described in James 2:15–16:

> If a brother or sister is without clothing and in need of daily food, and one of you says to them, "Go in peace, be warmed and be filled," and yet you do not give them what is necessary for their body, what use is that?

If a friend has a legitimate need, it is inappropriate merely to say, "Well, have a good attitude, and believe that God will take care of you." It's just not that simple.

GOD GIVES SPECIAL GRACE FOR SPECIAL PURPOSES

For me, being single has been *the most* challenging aspect of my Christian experience. Through various difficulties in life such as my dad's death when I was a teenager and significant physical problems, I have always experienced God's grace. He's always given me ways to cope and overcome challenges. But surmounting the challenges of being single has been in a whole different category than *any* other challenge. Because my relational needs continued to be insufficiently met regardless of the depth of my relationship with God, it seemed as if marriage was the only solution. I didn't see any adequate alternatives.

Yet, because God was not bringing marriage about, I asked for the grace needed to be truly victorious. I remember asking

God one day as I was rollerblading, "Where is Your grace, Father? Where is Your grace for *this*? Why can't I find what I need to overcome everything I'm feeling?" He didn't answer my question *that* day. But He's slowly been revealing the answer over the last few years.

I've learned that God's grace comes to us in different ways. Sometimes God's grace gives us power to endure a trial, and sometimes His grace gives us power to bring about change. The grace He gives depends on His purposes and what He's trying to achieve. He does this on an individual level and a corporate level. Let me illustrate this concept by example.

God gave many African Americans the grace to endure generations of discrimination and deplorable treatment by racists. He also gave Dr. Martin Luther King Jr. grace to lead a movement to awaken our nation to things it either did not see or did not want to see. In this historic development, God caught people's attention and got them to step outside the box of their culture and see its flaws. We look back now on the Civil Rights Movement and see that change was needed. It is so obvious now. God removed the blinders we had on. But there was a time when people didn't see it. It wasn't obvious. Before the blinders came off, African Americans longed for the open doors of opportunity whites enjoyed. But our culture made it much harder to walk through those doors and satisfy those longings.

Some parallels in this example illustrate the effect our culture has on us. I'm not suggesting that singles are mistreated in ways African Americans have been, but I am using parallels to depict concepts. We find it hard to have relational needs adequately met due to our culture, much as African Americans found it hard to have doors of opportunity opened due to the culture. Before the blinders came off, some thought the color of one's skin was the problem, but we later realized our culture was the problem.

Similarly, as certain blinders have remained on us, we think that not being married is the problem when, in actuality, the culture is more of a problem than we have realized. Our unmet desires leave us longing for something better—something we know is possible because we see others enjoying it. God in His goodness has given singles grace to endure living in a culture where our relational needs often are inadequately met. But I believe He also wants to grace visionaries like Dr. Martin Luther King Jr. who can see how the culture needs to change and who have faith to push for change.

The alternate ways God has to meet our relational needs have been submerged under our culture, and God wants to bring them soaring to the surface. He wants to make alternatives *much more* accessible, obvious and normative in our churches. Yes, you can experience a degree of satisfaction and fulfillment in the current culture, but I believe there is *so much more* God wants to open up to you to make life better. Much as God wanted and still wants to wipe away things in our culture that make life harder on African Americans, He wants to wipe away things that unnecessarily make life harder on singles. He wants to do away with the cultural impediments that make gaining and sustaining companionship and a sense of belonging difficult for us and to establish new ways of relating we haven't previously considered. But God doesn't pour new wine into old wineskins (Mark 2:22), so what "old wineskin" is He going to eliminate?

I believe He wants to eliminate the cultural division between singles and couples. He wants to address the strong sense of individualism in our broader culture that keeps us from living close enough to friends to enjoy regular interaction and a sense of support. And He wants to eliminate cultural mind-sets that prevent us from recognizing and seizing opportunities to plug in to our churches in diverse ways.

I believe the following scriptures describe the desire in God's heart to smooth the path for singles by addressing the cultural impediments:

> I will go before you and make the rough places
>   smooth;
> I will shatter the doors of bronze, and cut through
>   their iron bars.[1]

—ISAIAH 45:2

> And I will make my mountains into level paths for
> them. The highways will be raised above the valleys.

—ISAIAH 49:11, NLT

> I will even make a roadway in the wilderness.

—ISAIAH 43:19

God wants to make the path *easier*. I'm not suggesting that the church assume responsibility for seeing to it that you get connected—to make it happen for you. The church cannot do this *for* you. But it can promote an environment that more readily facilitates your ability to connect to others in a healthy and balanced way. Like so many other things about living life as a Christian, the church encourages each individual to take responsibility for himself or herself and make wise, godly choices. The church holds out signposts to say, "This is the way, walk ye in it" (Isa. 30:21, KJV).

To promote an environment that supports you connecting to others, your church must not only encourage you as an individual to take the steps necessary to connect, but must also promote this to the *whole* church. Why? Because many of us have worked diligently and tirelessly to "connect," but have experienced only minimal success. Perhaps this describes you. We are fighting an uphill battle that will not end until the *entire* church recognizes the legitimate need we have to feel connected to the whole church.

Our lives affect one another. None of us live on a relational island. Consequently, although we are not responsible *for* one another, we are responsible *to* one another.[2] We have to assess rightfully what our responsibilities to one another are, and then walk in that. As we do, we will more readily be able to develop the sense of belonging and connection that is needed for normal, healthy growth.

So start examining how you can remove impediments and start moving in some new directions. The first area to examine is singles ministry. This may come as a surprise, but if your church has a singles ministry, some impediments may actually spring from the way in which it is functioning in your church, which we'll discuss in the next chapter.

Chapter 12

Separation for Separation's Sake

One way the church does recognize and validate the genuine need of singles for companionship and belonging is through the traditional singles ministry model that many churches have adopted. But it falls short. Although this model, in some ways, truly can address and provide for some needs of singles, it has certain inherent flaws. We need to reevaluate this model, extract from it what is helpful and let the rest go. We also need to supplement the model with new approaches that more effectively reach the diverse spectrum of singles in today's church, especially singles beyond their early twenties.

We need a paradigm shift, not merely a program shift—a whole new approach, not a whole new program. This requires a new way of *thinking*, not merely a new way of *doing*. As hard as this might be for some to recognize or acknowledge, I believe we need to lay aside the idea that a church can adequately minister to *all* singles through the traditional singles ministry model.

Before going further, I need to explain what I mean by a "traditional singles ministry model." Typically, various types of functions specifically for singles are offered through a singles ministry. Usually this includes Bible study groups or other types of small fellowship groups, a variety of large group functions, which often include purely social functions, and a range of other programs for and with singles such as planned outings, annual conferences or retreats and service projects. Some have the objective of raising up leaders from amidst the church's singles. While many of these types of functions are good, the model through which they are offered does not adequately meet the needs of *all* singles and should not be viewed as doing so. It may work for those in their early twenties, but it holds problems for those beyond.

For a variety of reasons, many singles, after reaching their mid- to late-twenties, do not like and do not wish to be involved in their church's singles ministry. For example, the singles ministry of our church routinely attracted less than 5 percent of the total singles in our congregation regardless of who was in charge or how great the programs were. Yet many churches, out of a good and earnest desire to meet the needs of singles, continue to put a great deal of time and energy into their singles ministry. They may try a variety of approaches, hoping to discover the right approach that increases the turnout.

Sometimes pastors establish this type of ministry because singles in their church request it. It's natural for pastors to assume that those asking represent the desires of most singles. In reality, a majority of a church's singles may not actually be interested in having a singles ministry, but the pastor assumes they do because he or she is hearing only from the singles who vocalize their desire. It may simply be that the others are silent.

Another dynamic also occurs. Some people recognize that singles need *something*, but they are not sure what. They may approach a pastor stating that the church needs to provide *something* for singles. Visitors might also ask the pastor, "So, what do you have for singles?"

The pastor wants to have an answer! Seeking to meet these needs, the pastor may be inclined to think, *Well, we must get a singles ministry going.* It's easy to assume this because when it comes to meeting the needs of singles, it's the only model out there. There isn't a better alternative. Until now, there hasn't been a comprehensive plan that replaces it.

Pastors naturally turn to other churches to see what they are doing to meet the needs. The most obvious thing to observe is singles ministry. It is an obvious choice because it's program oriented. It can be studied, modified to fit a particular church and then implemented. It is somewhat tangible, making it easier to copy than an approach that is conceptual. So the model perpetuates itself because this is what singles and pastors see happening in various churches. They know that singles need *something*, and they can readily adopt this "solution" to address the problems. I'm suggesting we look outside the box and see something new and different. I believe the things I'm proposing will satisfy the "silent" singles as well as those who have enjoyed their singles ministry.

Before continuing, I'd like to share my testimony about how I came to advocate this paradigm shift. Some singles in my church approached me about getting more involved with our church's singles ministry. I was torn because I saw great need, but I also felt that the traditional singles ministry model wasn't the whole answer because I knew many singles who were not attracted to singles functions. Yet, I didn't have any alternatives to offer.

I earnestly sought God in prayer for answers—surely the God of the universe had a plan that would work. As I sought the Lord, ideas started to come. Among those ideas, a key one was that instead of ministering to singles separately, God wanted to minister to singles by blending them more into the church community. He wanted to bridge the gap between singles and couples, and He wanted to heal the wounds caused by this separation. I truly believe that the changes I'm calling for are borne out of God's heart.

As with all steps of faith, it is risky to suggest something new. It is also risky to explain why the existing model does not work for all singles. I think many people tiptoe around this issue because they don't want to offend anyone. I sincerely don't want to offend anyone either. People with great intentions and hearts of gold have worked sacrificially to put together singles ministries in their churches. Those who have done so have a heart for singles and are to be blessed, honored and commended. The paradigm shift I'm suggesting is not meant to take away from what they have done and are doing, but to come alongside them.

We want to reach the same end objectives—for singles to be cared for, to be blessed and to be a blessing. What I'm calling for should *complement* the work of existing leaders. If your church has a great ministry going, that's wonderful! But many churches do not have a vibrant and dynamic way of ministering to singles, and even among those that do, there are singles who do not feel comfortable in their church's singles ministry. They too need to feel like a true part of the church and should be valued and cared for whether involved in singles ministry or not.

It is not my intention to cause division by bringing this up. My goal is unity. By getting this issue out in the open, I think singles can become *more* unified. We won't have to distinguish ourselves as singles who support the singles ministry vs. those who do not involve themselves. Instead, we can be singles doing our unique part, whatever it may be, to serve and unify the whole church. It is tragic if we wound or discourage each other as if we are on opposing sides just because we have a different perspective. My sincere hope is that those who are devoted to the traditional singles ministry model will simply be open to my explanation regarding the perspective of other singles in the church.

I believe this perspective is needed by singles ministry leaders—especially those who have felt discouraged or hurt due to low turnout or what they perceive to be little support by others. Assumptions are sometimes made that the low turnout is a statement about the program, or worse, the leaders. Some leaders have been frustrated or disillusioned, believing low turnout to indicate apathy or lack of commitment on the part of the singles in their church. While these factors likely have some role in the attendance rate, they are not the only factors.

Low turnout should get our attention, though. When only a small percentage of a church's singles regularly participate in its singles ministry, the leaders should be asking, "What's wrong?"[1] I hope what I'm about to share helps answer that question and also soothes some of the frustration and hurt leaders have experienced. Lack of attendance is not always a statement about the leaders, the program or the commitment level of the singles. Other factors arise from the model itself, with its inherent flaws that cannot be overcome no matter how great the leaders or programs are, or how committed the singles are.

REASONS WHY SOME SINGLES DISLIKE ATTENDING SINGLES EVENTS

There are several reasons why a single may not find singles ministry events attractive. One reason is that a single may feel like he or she is going to a lonely heart's club, no matter how great the people are who attend the singles event. Why? Because let's face it—singles want fellowship. Some crave it. And we all know it.

Some singles are uncomfortable because by attending they think people will perceive them to be lonely. Whether the people attending actually *are* lonely is practically irrelevant; it's the *perception* that matters. The perception arises from the fact that the function is specifically for *singles*. While we wish this perception did not exist, we have to be realistic—for now, it does. The changes I believe God is bringing about will allow this perception to fade gradually. But for now, it's there, and we just can't get away from that.

Some singles feel very uncomfortable attending a singles event because they believe most attendees go with an underlying motive of finding a mate. Although nothing is wrong with having this motive (it's natural if you want to get married!), the underlying awareness of it, which you can hardly ignore, can easily make you feel like every man or woman there is checking you out.

Conversely, if you attend a friend's wedding, go to a church softball game or attend a conference, because you're in a *mixed* crowd, you don't feel overtly checked out. These are natural settings in which to meet others. The discomfort produced by the unseen yet felt awareness of underlying motives is absent. A singles event, in contrast, can feel contrived and awkward.

We can remember ourselves back at a high school dance when the primary thing on everyone's mind was trying to make the right maneuvers to get someone interested or to keep someone interested. While that may have felt normal in high school, to many it does not feel normal at twenty-eight or thirty-six or forty-two.

Yet many single Christians feel compelled to put themselves in this situation because it seems to be one of the only avenues they have to meet someone. If we are not going to do the bar scene, and if we are limiting our dating options only to Christians, well, where do we turn? I'll address that question later. For now, I just wanted to explain this aspect of why some singles avoid singles events.

Another problem created by the known underlying motive is that it heightens the potential for some to feel rejected. If you frequently attend singles events yet no one expresses interest in you, after a period of time, you can start to feel *really* rejected. You go home feeling badly and wondering, *What's wrong with me?*

An additional reason some singles avoid singles ministries is that there's something about joining a singles ministry that can make a single feel he or she is resigning to never be married—and most singles do not want to resign themselves to this. Perhaps one reason for this perception is the fact that some believe singles ministry represents a group of people who feel *called* to remain single. I suspect another reason is because most people join groups that are relevant to an enjoyable aspect of their lives that they desire to be ongoing. However, singles groups are comprised of people who share something in common that almost all of them wish to change.

If a single really dislikes being single, then he or she may not wish to belong to a group that constantly reminds him or her of the very thing he or she wishes not to be. For example, some people attend infertility groups. They long for the day they no longer need to attend the group because they are holding a baby in their arms. It's kind of a love-hate relationship. You may love the people and support, but you can't stand being reminded of that aspect of your life. You'd much rather have resolution to the issue that originally propelled you to join.

Some singles don't involve themselves in singles ministry because they are very busy doing other ministry work in areas where God has called and equipped them. For example, they may be highly involved in evangelistic efforts, children's ministry or ministry to the poor. These singles may feel they don't have enough time or energy to serve in another ministry. They should not be made to feel something is wrong with them because they are not involved specifically with the singles doing "singles ministry" but instead are active elsewhere. Unfortunately, I've seen this attitude conveyed by some singles. It's problematic when people look upon the singles ministry as something in which *all or most* singles should be involved.

Some singles feel that by joining singles ministry, they would be cutting themselves off from the larger life of the church, which is unappealing to them. They may desire relationships with a variety of people and do not want to be perceived as desiring to associate with singles only. Thus they avoid singles ministry so as not to be misperceived.

PROBLEMS IN A TRADITIONAL SINGLES MINISTRY

The traditional model not only generates these factors that can make singles ministry unattractive to some singles; it also can generate some problems.

Ever-changing group dynamics

There is an inherent instability in singles ministry caused by changing group dynamics as couples form, start dating and then leave the group. This can be especially challenging when the singles ministry leader is the one who begins dating and leaves the helm. *The very nature of single ministry fosters this ongoing revolving door.* People come with the hope of finding someone, and if they are successful, they leave. The singles who remain have to reshuffle themselves. If this happens too frequently, it can be heart wrenching for the ones who remain.

Eventually, the singles who have experienced this over and over find it difficult to open up and allow themselves to get close to newcomers and others, fearing that they too ultimately will leave. This is tragic when it happens, and it can be detrimental to singles in particular because they often don't have the rootedness couples generally enjoy. Stable and ongoing relationships are needed all the more in the life of a single, and yet this ministry model can foster the exact opposite. Singles who are aware of this inherent instability may shy away from involvement to avoid the potential fracturing they fear will occur.

A subgroup of singles

Another pitfall inherent to the model is that a singles ministry will often take on the character of a subgroup of singles. By so doing, it no longer attracts or represents *all* singles. Because there are many different stages of being single, each with its own unique set of issues, a "one-size-fits-all" type of singles ministry is ineffective.

Here's what can happen even though it is not intentional. Let's say a man in his mid-thirties begins to lead a singles group. It is not uncommon, then, for other thirty-something singles who attend singles events to be attracted to this leader due to his age. Pretty soon, this "singles ministry" looks like a mostly thirties singles group. If a single in his or her twenties or fifties shows up, that single may feel like a fish out of water.

Consequently, you may find yourself in a church that has a "singles ministry" you don't fit into, and yet, you find others in your church expecting you to get involved. This can be very frustrating and can leave singles feeling as if they don't fit in anywhere in the church. They don't fit in with the singles ministry and they don't fit in with couples. Where are they to go?

A separation mentality

The current model also can foster an ongoing separation mentality in the church. If a church takes great effort to promote its singles ministry, it may communicate a church philosophy that asserts singles *should* be involved with the singles ministry. It sends a message that the church's leadership believes that this is the primary place where singles ought to get "plugged in." Not only singles pick up on this, but couples do, too.

Many couples assume most singles want to be involved with singles ministry and that the singles ministry successfully addresses their issues. Not being single, not having attended singles functions and not understanding the kinds of things I am explaining here, it is natural that they would assume this. But this assumption is often wrong. All the more, then, the church leadership needs to be clear in its message. If a strong and clear message advocating the integration of singles is not expressed, then by default, the mere existence of a singles ministry tends to separate the singles out. This is sad when what singles need so much is to feel welcome and included in all respects.

The scenario is exacerbated when the church establishes a specific, high-profile marriage and family ministry. When the congregation sees the church establish the family ministry as its own distinct entity, and the singles ministry as its own distinct entity, a strong separation message is perceived. Overcoming this perception requires a clear articulation that this is *not* what the church is advocating. Such a message can be successfully conveyed, but few churches are sending that message, probably because they haven't seen the need to do so.

Let's encourage our pastors to enhance the environment for integration by clearly communicating that integration is an important objective. They can communicate this objective powerfully by doing something it seems most people have never thought of—actually linking family ministry with ministry to singles. These ministries need not be totally separate. They share common, related purposes. Let's encourage our pastors to prayerfully consider this.

SINGLES AS A SUBGROUP OF THE CHURCH

I want to depict something about the traditional singles ministry by contrasting it with these growing marriage and family ministries. Usually the mission of family ministries is to strengthen and support couples in their marriage and parenting skills so they can effectively fulfill the call of God on their lives and prepare their children to do likewise. This mission is accomplished by training couples to overcome the challenges common in marriage. Everyone seems to understand that although couples gather from time to time for such training, they are not sequestered as a subgroup of the church to achieve this goal. In stark contrast, however, when we say, "singles ministry," it evokes an image of a subgroup of the church—namely singles—doing Bible studies, service projects and outings with singles only. We could instead follow the model of the family ministry and accomplish the mission of training singles to overcome their unique challenges by similarly gathering them from time to time for specific training. Beyond such training, we could encourage singles to be as integrated as couples throughout the church. Then we would not be fostering an environment where singles feel like they are *supposed* to look primarily just to other singles for most of their social and spiritual involvement.

The approach of setting apart singles into their own distinct subgroup springs out of two obvious ways that the needs of singles differ from couples. The means to satisfy relational needs differ. As a general rule, a couple's relational needs are met largely through their family and often through a wide variety of other social contexts. This is often not true of singles, at least not to the same degree. Thus, the approach of gathering all the singles together stems from a sincere desire to meet their relational needs. This approach is understandable, but too limiting. We need to promote more diverse channels through which singles can satisfy their legitimate relational needs. Those needs don't have to be met in a group that is primarily or entirely comprised of just singles.

If we're honest, I think we create a subgroup context—again, in stark contrast to the marriage and family ministry—because an underlying motive really is to provide an environment where singles can meet other singles and hopefully find their future spouses. Obviously, couples don't need that environment. There are other ways for singles to meet and mingle—ways that have the potential to be more successful because the setting is more natural and comfortable, not so contrived and obvious. As the church becomes more integrated, mingling will happen more frequently. As more friendships are formed across marital lines, there will be more opportunities for networking. Lots of *better* options for facilitating ways for singles to meet lie dormant now and need to be awakened! Heavy reliance on singles ministry to fulfill this purpose is, in part, the reason why we haven't looked to other, better ways.

Another contributing factor for creating a separated subgroup context for singles is that some singles feel uncomfortable around couples and prefer to disengage from them. Some assume couples don't want them around. Some don't want to subject themselves to insensitive comments from couples. Some think couples automatically view them as a threat to the couple's marriage. Some don't want to face the reminders of what they don't have—a spouse and children. While I understand these issues, I believe that singles who feel this way are really missing out on some priceless experiences. These impediments to integration can be addressed and resolved, which we'll discuss later.

Some churches may liken the separation aspect of singles ministry to the church's women's or men's ministry. However, we can't validate the separated approach we take to singles by comparing it to women's or men's ministry for two reasons. First, women want to be women. Men want to be men. Unlike singles, they are not hoping to change their status. Second, while women's ministries and men's ministries may hold events only for the participants in their respective ministries, it is clear that we don't separate men or women off unto themselves as a subgroup of the church. They are well integrated into the church as a whole.

APPROPRIATE CONTEXTS FOR TARGETING EVENTS SPECIFICALLY FOR SINGLES

This is *not* to say that there is never an appropriate occasion for separate events specifically for singles. For example, our church hosts what we call the "Single Parents' Fair." We provide free services such as legal assistance, health services, haircuts and oil changes to single parents in recognition of the financial hardships they often face. We do this to demonstrate love and support for single parents in our church and surrounding community. This event targets a need that is *specific* to these singles. There is an obvious reason for targeting the function to singles exclusively. Couples in our church are highly involved in this function. Thus, while helping single parents, we also foster unity between couples and singles!

Many things currently offered exclusively to singles in some churches could just as easily be open to all people, both married and single. For example, there need not be an exclusive singles' walking club, singles' finance ministry, singles' dinner club or singles' worship service. When these "generic" activities, which could be done in an integrated context, are offered exclusively to singles, it *heightens* the perception that the primary underlying reason for this exclusive setting is so that singles will meet and hopefully "match." Or it heightens the perception that singles and couples don't want, or don't know how, to mix. Neither perception promotes positive results.

When, however, we offer singles events having an obvious purpose that is unique to singles, that *purpose* becomes the focus, allowing the negative perceptions to fall aside. For example, I've been teaching seminars on issues unique to singles in walking out the Christian life, so the reason for targeting singles for this type of function is obvious. (By the way, even though the subjects are targeted to singles, couples are encouraged to attend these seminars too in an effort to increase their awareness of issues faced by singles. Our marriage and family pastor has attended, and his presence also encourages singles—it speaks loudly of his genuine interest. This is another step in the process of tearing down walls between couples and singles.)

The caveat, however, is that until a church makes a new approach clear, many singles will not attend a singles event even when the purpose for targeting singles is obvious and sensible. I know, because this is what they've told me. This demonstrates the power of the long-standing stigma some singles attach to "singles ministry." As we implement changes, I believe that stigma will gradually fade. Until then, we must utilize alternative means of providing useful information to singles about issues they face. One of many reasons why we need our pastors to teach about singles issues from the pulpit is precisely because singles need the information and training, but many will never go to a singles event to get it.

The bottom line is this: For our churches to promote successfully the integration of singles into the church at large, they need to stop separating singles unto themselves when there is no obvious and healthy purpose for that separation. When singles or couples support the continuation of something that is not helpful to singles, they foster continuing division in the church.

Deal with the real problem; don't skirt around it by fostering an environment that allows it to go unconfronted and unchanged. This approach doesn't help singles or couples. Instead of promoting separation, let's work together to give everyone—couples and singles—the opportunity to experience the blessings that come from involvement with each other. Let's not promote separation out of fear that singles will be left with nothing if we don't at least give them singles ministry, especially if this fear is fueled by a presumption that couples are aloof to the needs of singles. Instead, let's address the real problems.

A Better Way—Ministry *to* Singles

After all this, you may be asking, "So is there any room left for singles ministry?" I think there is, but it needs to be done in a different manner. The sole purpose should be to address the issues that are specific to singles. Events should be open, not exclusive. This way, all the pastors get involved, not just the singles pastor. Couples with a heart to better understand and come alongside singles are welcome. Thus the door is wide open for interaction. This promotes better communication between couples and singles, from which both derive benefits. For example, never-married singles can be mentored in marriage and parenting, and couples can likewise glean things from singles, like how to lean into God more than their spouse in difficulty.

To successfully shift to a new model of ministry to singles, we need to encourage our pastors and other church leaders to communicate clearly to the church that ministry to singles occurs in this open and integrated type of context, not in the old way. A loud and clear message is needed because the current mind-sets about what constitutes "singles ministry" are so ingrained. Encourage your church leaders to express the church's overall view of singles and their multifaceted involvement in the church. Unless your leaders clearly demonstrate the desire to meet the needs of singles in a *variety* of ways, when the congregation hears references to groups or events that *sound* like the old "singles ministry," they'll just assume everything is the same as always. They will not realize that your church has adopted a new approach, one that encourages specific training aimed at singles issues *and* the overall integration of singles.

We should probably call this new approach something else too, because using the term *singles ministry* tends to make everyone, singles and couples alike, think that just because it exists, it's the *primary* place of belonging for *all* singles, which isn't true. We should use terminology that does not create the impression that it's exclusive to singles—they lead, they teach, they gather, etc. Instead we want to convey that singles are the *subject* of the ministry but not necessarily the only ones by and for whom the ministry is offered. It is ministry *to* singles about things they face.

Personally, I almost always use the term "ministry to singles" instead of "singles ministry" because I believe this better reflects the true intent. It might seem like a small change in terminology, but this change helps convey that ministry to singles can be offered by anybody, married or single.

Another benefit gained under this new model is that someone like me, for example, who is involved as a single, can continue involvement even after marrying. This is such an advantage! It eliminates the inherent instability caused by the old mind-set whereby a person disengages from ministry to and with singles after he or she gets married.

In all these changes, your church doesn't have to do away with the fun, recreational types of activities and gatherings that

you and other singles enjoy. If you enjoy those types of functions, you can organize those events just as friends normally do
with one another! Pick a day, time and event, and spread the
word among friends. Make flyers with maps if you want to.
Singles, *as individuals*, are perfectly capable of organizing these
types of things on their own and do not need the church to
sponsor and arrange these events for them.

If an individual or group of friends plan an event and invite
only singles, this is vastly different than when the church does
so. We respect the concept of freedom of association. As individuals, we're free to decide whom we want to invite to parties
and other social gatherings. But the minute *the church* sponsors
an event and makes it for singles only, it is a different matter
altogether. Let's take the church out of it and do what friends
do naturally—plan and organize our own social gatherings.
This has a wholly different feel to it, and singles who currently
disdain singles ministry functions might be more inclined to go
to something that instead just feels like a friend's party.

All of these changes create a win-win situation for everybody. The singles ministry leaders who enjoy training can
continue on, because we need training. Singles who specifically enjoy singles ministry as it currently exists will still have
a variety of events tailored to them. And you can continue
your socializing by taking it into your own hands. If other
singles do not care to associate themselves specifically with
ministry to singles, they can receive adequate training
through broader avenues—for example, through sermons—
and can continue involvement in other areas of ministry in the
church. Additionally, by the church's overall increased attention to singles in general, *all* singles, both those who minister
specifically to singles and those who do not, can feel much
more cared for and valued. Everybody wins, and no one has to
be left out. Surely this is God's heart.

If your church adopts the paradigm shift I'm laying out—
this comprehensive new way of ministering to singles—I

believe you and other singles will thrive in ways you have not heretofore.

Now, let's turn to the next area for examination to see how we can continue to tear down additional obstacles and build up new avenues for relationships to form. Let's bring down the wall between singles and couples.

Chapter 13

Bridging the Great Divide

We've identified some aspects of the traditional singles ministry model that can hinder singles from connecting more fully to the church and from having our relational needs better met. If we "tear down" the elements of singles ministry that separate singles from the church generally and from couples specifically, we will take a step toward opening the doors to more diverse ways of meeting the legitimate relational needs of singles—all singles. Additional impediments must also be torn down. The next one we're going to look at is the wall between singles and couples.

Generally, the social circle of singles diminishes as we age and friends marry. The gap between singles and couples distances singles from half the population, cutting the pool from which old friends are kept and new friends are made. We singles feel this more deeply, because we don't have one primary person—a spouse—who is meeting many of our needs for companionship. Couples have the benefit of enjoying each other *and* having their social circle doubled by their spouse's friends and family. Meanwhile, the exact opposite occurs for us.

The gap also hinders our experience of community within the church body. If a church feels like a "couples church," singles may struggle with feeling welcome at special "all church" functions, such as picnics and covered-dish dinners. We may feel that we don't fit in because those types of functions are family centered. Some choose to stay away, despite the fact they likely want to feel a part of it all. Or, if many or most home groups are comprised primarily of couples, singles may shy away from those groups. It may not be because they do not wish to be a part of those groups, but because they feel they do not fit in. Singles who do not like attending singles functions can feel even more isolated. They don't want to be separated out with just other singles, and they may not feel that they fit in with couples. They can be doubly challenged.

At present, there don't seem to be many couples who know how to "pull" singles toward them in ways that make us feel comfortable and welcome. So we're left with this *repeating cycle*. It is going to take work on the part of both singles and couples to overcome this. We need to be willing to "push" our way in, so to speak, despite feeling out of place. Couples need to be willing to "pull" singles in and expand their own dimensions beyond family life.

GOD SETS THE SOLITARY IN FAMILIES

Let's talk about tearing down the wall between singles and couples and building bridges instead. Scripture indicates that the existing wall is not on God's blueprint, but that He is the Architect of a beautiful bridge! One of the most obvious passages to illustrate God's heart on this matter is in Psalm 68:6, which says, "God sets the solitary in families" (NKJV). The New American Standard reads, "God makes a home for the lonely."

I don't believe this is limited to the provision of adoption and foster homes for orphans or nursing homes for the elderly. Nor is it only addressing the homeless. Who are the solitary ones? Those of us without a spouse or children are solitary. We whose siblings and parents are spread across the nation or world are solitary. One person in four is especially "solitary," living alone. In some metropolitan areas, almost half the population lives alone![1]

Despite filling our schedules with many responsibilities and commitments, the bottom line is that at the beginning and ending of every day, many Christian singles get up and go to bed alone. We eat many meals alone. Much of life is spent alone.

BIBLICAL EXAMPLES OF
SINGLES SET IN FAMILIES

Scripture points to God's design to set the solitary in families not only in Psalm 68:6, but also through examples and exhortations in the Bible. One of the most touching examples God has given us is the account of Jesus making provision for His mother shortly before He died on the cross. This is what we find in John 19:26–27:

> When Jesus therefore saw His mother, and the disciple whom He loved standing nearby, He said to His mother, "Woman, behold, your son!" Then He said to the disciple, "Behold, your mother!" And from that hour, the disciple took her into his own household.

What a clear example that God does not want us to be on our own.

Another thing we see from Jesus' life is that even though His mother and other relatives were still alive, and He was not totally bereft of family, He had a special "family-like" relationship with Mary, Martha and Lazarus. Jesus, as a single man, was ministered to by being meaningfully included in the lives of these two sisters and their brother. (See John 11:1–44; 12:1–3; Luke 10:38–41; Matthew 26:7–13.)

Then there are Ruth and Naomi. Naomi, upon losing her husband, decided to return to her hometown. Ruth, Naomi's widowed daughter-in-law, had no obligation to accompany Naomi, but still she chose to leave her own hometown and return with Naomi. Ruth was faithful to Naomi, and when she remarried, she continued to treat Naomi as her beloved mother-in-law, though the actual family relationship had changed. Ruth later gave birth to a boy, and Naomi was just like a grandmother to him, though technically he was not her grandson. Ruth 4:16 says, "Naomi took care of the baby and cared for him as if he were her own" (NLT). The nature of Naomi's relationship to this new family is depicted in these words spoken by neighbors: "Naomi has a son" (v. 17, NIV). This is yet another tender story of how God took care of two single women—how He provided a "family" for both of them.

The Books of 1 Samuel and 2 Samuel tell the story of King David caring for Jonathan's son Mephibosheth after Jonathan died. (See 1 Samuel 20:14–15, 17, 23, 42; 2 Samuel 9:1–13; 21:7.) These passages further illustrate God setting the solitary in families. In Luke 1:39–56, Mary, a single woman, turned to Elizabeth and Zacharias, a married couple, in her time of need.

These giants of the faith demonstrate the beautiful vision of grafting singles more into our families. I don't think it is any coincidence that God chose to demonstrate these principles through such strong Bible figures.

Jesus further expanded the definition of *family* when He made it clear that we are related to Him as family through obedience to the Father: "Whoever does the will of My Father who is in heaven, he is My brother and sister and mother" (Matt 12:50). He also told us we are related to one another as family through our relationship to Him:

> There is no one who has left house or brothers or sisters or mother or father or children or farms, for My sake and for the gospel's sake, but that he shall receive a hundred times as much now in the present age, houses and brothers and sisters and mothers and children…
>
> —MARK 10:29–30

The Bible also speaks of the deep value in friendship, sometimes even in contrast to family ties. Proverbs 18:24 says, "There is a friend who sticks closer than a brother." Proverbs 17:17 states, "A friend loves at all times, and a brother is born for adversity." Proverbs 27:10 reads this way in the Amplified Bible, "Your own friend and your father's friend, forsake them not; neither go to your brother's house in the day of your calamity. Better is a neighbor who is near [in spirit] than a brother who is far off [in heart]."

So we can see from biblical biographies and passages that God would like singles and families to benefit from one another, especially within the broader family that we call our spiritual family. But today's cultural gap between couples and singles prevents this from happening to the extent it could. Are you aware of this gap? Consider the following questions:

- Do you have any close friends who are married?

- If you do have some married friends, do they have other single friends, or are you an anomaly in their social circle?

- Does it seem that many social get-togethers among those you know tend to be mostly all singles or, conversely, mostly all couples?

- Does your church offer ongoing, long-term Bible study groups or other types of long-term small groups that are exclusively for couples or exclusively for singles? Does it offer many other functions to just singles or just couples?

- Would you feel comfortable inviting a couple out to get pizza with you and some of your single friends? Do couples periodically ask you over for dinner or to watch a video?

I'm not suggesting that this gap runs the full gamut of activities and functions in the church. Singles and couples do work shoulder to shoulder in various ministries—for example, in the worship ministry, children's ministry or ministry to the homeless. But few of these connections go deeper than the superficial level of mere acquaintances serving together.

UNITY WITH DIVERSITY

Because of this separation, both the church corporately and we as individuals are missing out on things God desires for us, both married and single. Division means less strength and effectiveness in extending the kingdom of God. Not only are we missing out and missing the mark, but we also are unintentionally and needlessly hurting each other. The church would be so much healthier if the walls that divide us were broken down. The walls will fall through understanding and, in some instances, repentance. Repentance is often the first step toward healing and reconciliation.

God has made it clear to us, both in Scripture and experientially, that He wants His church to be united. Jesus prayed, "That they may all be one; even as Thou, Father, art in Me, and I in Thee, that they also may be in Us; that the world may believe that Thou didst send Me" (John 17:21; see also Eph. 2:14–22; 4:3; Phil. 2:1–4).

God calls for this unity amidst great diversity. He loves diversity! We see this in all His vast creation. And we see the unity He longs for within this diversity powerfully depicted in Revelation when people "from every nation and all tribes and peoples and tongues" will worship God together (Rev. 7:9–10). The unity we have through our relationship to Jesus is enough of a common bond to do away with things that divide us.

> There is neither Jew nor Greek, there is neither slave nor free man, there is neither male nor female; for you are all one in Christ Jesus.
>
> —Galatians 3:28

Let's work on "neither single nor married" within His church, because currently, we don't seem like one whole family. Whenever we are missing the mark, there will be hurt and unfortunate consequences. Jesus said that you will know a tree by its fruit (Matt. 7:17; 12:33; Luke 6:43). I believe the fruit produced by the existing division between couples and singles proves it is not God's best and highest for us.

I'll give you some examples of the wall's effects that I have seen. These examples are a microcosm of what is happening on a grander scale. I know of a single mom in a home group

comprised of both singles and couples. The couples of this
home group made it a point to sit together at church services.
But outside of the context of the actual group meetings, this
single mom felt like an outsider. She was not comfortable sitting with them, so she didn't.

That's the bad news, but here's the good news. It so happened that I had what I believe was a God-ordained conversation one evening with the leader of that group, explaining
many of the concepts included in this book. I was not aware of
the situation with this single mom, and neither was the leader.
After our conversation, this leader was truly moved in his heart
to bring about change in his group. During the next meeting,
he shared his thoughts and apologized to any singles there who
had felt left out. That's when he found out about how this single mom had been feeling. She started weeping as he talked;
she later described her experience. Great healing came. The
leader's eyes were opened, the group's eyes were opened, and
now that single mom is no longer "on the fringes."

I know of a single man who complained that the married
couples in his home group would often get together socially
outside of the group meetings, and although he had a really
good rapport with those folks, they never thought to include
him in those other events. He was hurt.

Things like that have happened to me too, including something even more obvious. For years I was unable to attend a
particular home group attended by five couples with whom I
was good friends. Because of my friendships and the location,
it would have been quite natural for me to attend this group,
but I could not. Why? It was a couples-only home group.
Now, I fully support home groups whose purpose is to focus
on marriage—for a *season*. After *several years*, however, when
the group *no longer is focusing solely on marriage*, I can't see a
justification based on principle to continue excluding singles.[2]

The reverse is also true, based on principle, regarding
ongoing singles-only groups. I know some people who have

been caught in the awkward position of having to tell someone on the opposite side of the marital line that he or she
cannot attend the group. This can be especially disconcerting
when you are forced to turn away a nonbelieving friend who
finally expresses an interest in meeting these wonderful
people you've talked about so much!

This exclusion seeps beyond merely the group meeting.
For example, at an all-church function, it's common for
people of the same home group to congregate or gravitate to
one another. The exclusive nature of the group acts as an
invisible "boundary" even at the all-church function so that
people on the opposite side of the marital line don't feel comfortable crossing the "boundary." This is a very important
point because it seems there is a growing trend toward developing these segregated home groups. I recently visited a
church and observed the display of information concerning
their regular home groups (not special, short-term groups). I
counted two groups that were clearly open to both couples
and singles; six that were designated "neighborhood," so
apparently those also were mixed; none for singles only; and
twenty-five for couples only!

I *know* the types of things I've described are not done mali-
ciously or with even the slightest intent to hurt. I'm *certain* that
none of the couples involved in any of the above-referenced
instances had any idea of the hurt that was being caused. They
were simply blind to it. The blindness is caused by existing
mind-sets—mind-sets that need to change. As these change,
our church culture will change, opening up more avenues for
singles to feel connected.

Couples have been hurt too, not just singles. I've talked
with a lot of married people who have expressed consternation
over trying to remain friends with singles. They don't want to
leave us in the lurch. They feel bad about this. They wonder
how we will feel around them. They're not sure if being with
them serves as a hard reminder to us of what we wish we had.

They feel faced with a lose/lose situation—they fear they will hurt their single friends whether they include or exclude us. Some couples agonize over this. For others, it is not so much this issue, but more the fact that they get to a place where they don't know how to help their single friends anymore. Time marches on, the friend is still single, and his or her struggle may be escalating. They hurt so much for the friend but feel helpless.

WE ARE ONE BODY

The church is fractured and thus weakened. Jesus said, "If a house is divided against itself, that house will not be able to stand" (Mark 3:25). Tragically, some "houses" (churches) have fallen, caused in part by the loss of too many singles who either left or decided not to attend in the first place.[3] Others that remain "standing" are weakened by the loss of some fantastic talent and commitment of the singles who leave.[4] Despite this quiet exodus, I don't think Christians necessarily view the church as fractured by this issue because the division isn't intentional or malicious.

However, compared to the way God wants things to be, we are fractured. This is an instance where we think we're OK until God shows us His way, a higher and better way. "There is a way which *seems right* to a man, but its end is the way of death" (Prov. 16:25, emphasis added). In Isaiah 55:8–9 we read:

> "For My thoughts are not your thoughts,
> Neither are your ways My ways," declares the LORD.
> "For as the heavens are higher than the earth,
> So are My ways higher than your ways,
> And My thoughts than your thoughts."

God has a better way for the church to go, and it is a way in which we can be healed from the "death" that has resulted from walking blind regarding this issue.

When you think about natural families, it is a bit easier to see how the church is fractured. In a family you have young, old, married, single, disabled or not, rich, poor. You are bound together because you are family, and that transcends the differences between you. Families are healthier because of the blending of their differences. For example, the young need the old, and the old need the young. Think of a grandfather lighting up over his grandchildren. Think of a frazzled mom calling her own mom for help! In the reverse, unfortunately, we've probably all seen or heard what happens when family members get left out of the circle, right? Their feelings are hurt. And so it is with us as Christ's family.

Not only are we fractured, but also we don't care for one another as we should—as God has called us to. We are a "many membered body," each with different gifts, talents and abilities. We've been given gifts that differ so that the body will be able to care for itself. Paul says in Romans 12:4–5, "For just as we have many members in one body and all the members do not have the same function, so we, who are many, are one body in Christ, and individually members one of another." He stresses the same thing in 1 Corinthians 12:21 and 25 when he uses the analogy of the body:

> The eye cannot say to the hand, "I have no need of you"; or again the head to the feet, "I have no need of you"…there should be no division in the body, but that the members should *have the same care* for one another.
>
> —EMPHASIS ADDED

We are part of one another. That's why it also says, "And if one member suffers, all the members suffer with it; if one member is honored, all the members rejoice with it" (1 Cor. 12:26). Instead, some of us can't rejoice with the new bride or the new mother, or we resent being asked to pray for the infertile couple. (And I understand this—I've been there—but it's not right.) I also see married couples who are oblivious to the suffering endured by many singles who really want to get married and have children, or who are struggling after divorce.

There is also an issue about us providing "the *same* care for one another." I've watched families rally around one another in time of need when, for example, babies are born or spouses are away or a mom is sick. It is wonderful to see the body of Christ function in this way! However, generally I have not observed a similar type of rallying for singles, and I think it's probably because there are not more commonly held experiences to which couples relate and respond to out of empathy.

Another reason is that many families in the church tend to network well with one another, but without strong ties to singles, this networking between singles and couples is not strong. We need to sensitively help couples understand that, for example, when a single living alone becomes very ill, he or she can be in as much or more need as a sick mom. Even though caring for children is not an issue, that single has absolutely no one there unless friends offer to come over to help. There is no spouse who could come home from work if necessary. *I don't share this to solicit pity for singles.* I'm not looking for that, and I'm sure other singles aren't either. I'm only highlighting an area of weakness that we can encourage the church to shore up. Oversights of this nature are not intentional; until now, the church just generally hasn't seen it. God can use us to gently, lovingly, humbly open blind eyes. We must be careful in so doing that we are not removing a speck from someone else's eye while there's a log in our own (Matt. 7:4)!

As long as this gap continues, the church will not be reflecting the body of Christ to the world in the manner God intended. "By this all men will know that you are My disciples, if you have love for one another" (John 13:35). When our non-Christian coworkers, friends or neighbors witness this gap, what does that say about the church? Many non-Christians, even in our postmodern society, seem to know intuitively that the church claims to be a family of believers, united in Christ. But then they see this reality, and our actions speak louder than words. We know some of our non-Christian friends believe we'd be more socially connected if we'd hang out at the local hot spots (often bars) rather than at church. In some ways, the church is less supportive of singles than social circles outside the church. This is a liability when it comes to reaching out to those who don't know the Lord, especially those who are single. The church has an opportunity to demonstrate a distinctive difference to the world. My prayer is that we seize it.

The pastor of my church (a church of over six thousand) asked me to share a bit about my vision and hope that our church would build more bridges between couples and singles. The comments later made to me spoke volumes about this issue of division. Some who had been divorced shared their pain with me. They explained that even though many friendships stayed intact at a heart level after their divorce, they were no longer included in typical social events. And this at a time they most needed the fellowship of those friends. Younger singles also talked to me. They talked of the pain of being left behind as their single friends married.

There were happy reports, too. One married woman told me she was sitting with a single friend at the service when I spoke. After my talk, the two friends made a commitment to keep working at their friendship despite the challenges presented by the differences in their lifestyles. Another woman was there with a sister who was single. They wept together as I shared with the congregation. They were so glad someone was finally encouraging us to become more integrated. Many couples said to me afterward, "We've needed to hear this for a long time." The positive response was overwhelming! People's hearts are in the right place; we just need our eyes to be opened.

Over time, as God does His work in this area, I believe we will watch Him bring conviction, which will lead to repentance on the part of both couples and singles over the hurt that has come through this unfortunate division. I also believe that from that repentance, God will bring about much deep healing. My prayer is that God will use this book as a spark to light a fire of repentance where it is needed.

As you read on, think of your reading as one of the steps toward bringing increased understanding that will lead to healing. The more you understand about this issue and God's view of it, the better equipped you will be for God to use you as a change agent in His church! Equip yourself. You may feel that I'm preaching to the choir by writing this to singles. You may think, *Yes, this is great you are admonishing us in this way, but couples need to hear it as well.* I understand that. Who are they going to hear it from? YOU! Who is going to model it for them? YOU! Share your heart about these things in a sincere manner. Set an example by walking toward couples instead of away. Extend a hand of friendship. Start building bridges between couples and singles.

Does the task seem too big? We serve a God who does the impossible. Do you feel that you are only one person, so what real difference can you make? Abraham was only one person, as were Moses and David. Jesus turned the world upside down with only twelve men. Start somewhere, and watch what God can do through your life! If every person reading this builds even just one bridge with a family, think of the difference in the church! By every effort you make to bridge the gap, you please and glorify God, and the church is blessed and strengthened.

Chapter 14

Bridge Building 101

So how did we get here anyway? What has caused this gap to exist? The reasons vary for couples and singles and change over time.

In our twenties, many couples form and proceed on to marriage. In this stage, we need to step aside, to a healthy degree, from our friends who are dating to let those relationships flourish. Couples in this stage also begin to pull away more unto themselves as their relationship grows. If the relationship remains serious and proceeds to marriage, often the couple begins to associate more with other couples and less with their friends who remain single. This is where the gap begins, and it widens as time progresses.

The differences in the lifestyle of couples and singles make it harder to remain friends. It becomes easier and easier to let those once meaningful relationships slip away. To some extent, this is part of life. People grow and change. Some friendships are for a season of life. But the bigger problem is that as individuals collectively repeat this cycle, this pattern becomes a rut we fall into without realizing it. As time has passed, the rut has become so deep, so ingrained, that we don't seem to recognize the value in remaining connected across marital lines.

And so, for example, when people in midlife become single either through divorce or a spouse's death, they experience the shock that occurs in their social circle. Where they were accustomed to socializing with other couples, suddenly they are thrust into what can feel like "no-man's land" as their relationships with couples drop off. Because this separation has become the societal norm, bridging the gap on a personal level is made more difficult.

Before I continue, I want to make three things clear. First, I'm not implying that there aren't *any* good relationships between singles and couples. You may have some good friends who are married. Your friendship with them is, however, more the exception rather than the general rule within the church. We need friendships that span across marital lines to become more normative. When they do, you will feel more supported in the family-based friendships you already may have and in the new ones you form. ("Family-based friendship" is a term I use to convey the concept of a friendship between a single and a family.)

Second, some of your friendships may be with just one married spouse, as opposed to friendship with that spouse's entire family. These friendships are also good, and we need to see more of them as well. Your social interaction in these relationships is more likely to fall along the lines of periodic nights "out with the guys" or "girls night out." While I wholly endorse those types of friendships, my discussion below addresses a different type of friendship connection—one that encompasses the entire family.

Third, what I'm about to share about family-based friendships is not meant to minimize the significance of your friendships with other singles or those of couples with other couples. Those are wonderful in a different way, and they are much needed, too. For example, it's nice to talk with another single who understands, from experience, many of the things I find challenging as a single without me having to explain them. The same principle applies to friendships between married persons. It's best if we have a mixture of friendships with both married people and singles. So while I focus our attention here on integrated friendships between singles and families, I'm not diminishing the importance of friendships with others of the same marital status.

SEPARATION FACTORS FOR SINGLES

Various factors foster the separation of singles and couples. One of the foremost reasons why we want to run away from couples is because of what I call the "*pain of reminders*." That is, by being with a couple and their children, you come face to face with what you do not have—a spouse and, likely, children too—and it can be painful to be reminded of what you are missing. It can be hard when you observe the exchange of even simple affection between a husband and wife. It can be hard for singles without children to witness the incredible bond parents have with their children. Even little things can trigger pain, like watching a child be "measured up" on his or her birthday to see how much he or she has grown in a year. This is a reminder that this family is building a history together, having a future that will continue to expand and bonds that will grow stronger with the years. It can be easy in those moments for you to contrast this with your life, which may not *seem* to hold such promise and which, in contrast, *at that time*, seems barren. That's painful. This certainly is not the fault of the couple, by any means; it's just reality.

Another reason we separate ourselves from couples is that we easily feel like a "third wheel" around couples. It's an awkward feeling, and we want to avoid it as much as possible.

We also may feel unwanted by a friend's spouse or family. Because of the existing gap, it is easy to *assume* that you have no place or value in the life of someone else's family. Or worse, you may think that a family would view you as a drain.

Some singles don't mix with married people because they simply don't see *why* it is good to have married friends. If no reason compels you in this direction, you have no reason to seek it out, to make it a reality.

SEPARATION FACTORS FOR COUPLES

On the other side of the fence, some couples may not mix with singles because they don't think singles want to hang out with a "boring married couple." They are still picturing life as a single the way they remember it. They think of the carefree, independent days of frequent get-togethers with other singles. With this mind-set, it is easy for them to assume no single would want to enter into the responsibility-laden life of a family. Similarly, couples may truly have great difficulty believing that we actually desire to spend time with their children, especially in the context of what may feel like chaos to the couple.

Another factor is that it simply might feel odd to a couple to invite a single or two along on a family outing, and they can easily assume we have no interest.

Many of the things that families do revolve around the commitments and interests of their children. Parents attend a lot of sporting events, plays, recitals and the like. Some of these events, to the parents, seem more obligatory than something they eagerly do. For the love of their children, they go. With this perspective, it surely does not dawn on them that you might enjoy joining them.

Often parents make quite a few social decisions based on the friendships their children form. If parents know that their children will jump at the chance to visit certain families or have certain families over because they really enjoy the children, parents can easily be more inclined to initiate social events with these families. However, unless you do a good job of developing relationships with the children of your married friends, those children may not be as interested in you if you have no children. This certainly may influence the decisions of their parents.

Unless a married person experienced a significant period of singleness before marriage or has been divorced or widowed, he or she has no reference point to understand what you may face as a single. Your needs are not intuitively obvious, so some couples don't extend a hand of friendship merely because they don't realize your need of it.

On the other hand, some couples *do* know the needs of singles but are uncertain how to help. They may fear that inviting a single to join their family may be like pouring salt in the wound. Or, in knowing the depth of needs, some may feel overwhelmed, viewing what they offer as only a drop in the bucket. Or they may feel inept to minister effectively to singles whom they know to be in great pain.

GENERAL REASONS FOR THE GAP

There are some general reasons for this gap that can be experienced by either a single or a married person. An obvious reason is that commonalities draw people together, so the differences between a couple's lifestyle and a single's lifestyle tend to foster separation. Additionally, people naturally follow familiar patterns. It seems that the main reason these types of friendships haven't happened with greater regularity is simply because we haven't seen them modeled much. We don't know what they *look* like. And due to lack of understanding, we haven't been convinced of the need. It takes something quite compelling for people to look outside the box and develop new patterns of relating.

Envy of the benefits both singles and couples perceive the other has also fosters separation. I'm referring here to the "grass is always greener on the other side of the fence" mentality. For example, couples may envy the freedom they think you have, and you may envy the full life you perceive a family has. Where envy exists, separation often exists.

Various fears can also hinder friendships between couples and singles. A couple may fear a single will become too dependent upon them for fellowship and a sense of family. You may fear the same for yourself. Couples may see a relationship with a single person as a threat to their marriage, depending upon the sense of security they have in their marriage. Even if there is no real threat, if there *appears* to be, this will separate a single from a couple. Some singles simply *assume* the married

person of their same sex automatically will be jealous if they try
to extend a hand of friendship. Are you gifted with children?
Sometimes a parent who has insecurities about his or her parenting abilities may consider you a threat, particularly if their
children grow quite close to you.

Couples and singles also may struggle with drawing healthy
boundaries. A couple may wonder how they should keep their
family identity distinct from a single friend who becomes like
a surrogate aunt or uncle. Or a single may wonder how to keep
from feeling used as a convenient babysitter by the couple. A
single or married person may have concerns about whether
their extended family members will understand and accept the
"family-like" relationship they have with a family or a single.
These are all valid issues you must deal with in order to successfully forge healthy relationships across marital lines.

Now that we are aware of a gap, know why it is harmful and
understand how we got here, how do *we get rid of it? How do we
build bridges?* Since an entire book could be written on this subject alone, for brevity's sake I will hit only the high points.

BUILDING BRIDGES

One motivator for bringing about any change in life is first to
see the benefits of the change. So, one step in ridding ourselves
of this gap is to catch the vision of all God has for us if we do
build bridges. We need a sense of what the replacement looks
like and why it's good. Like any friendship, God has something
good in store for both parties.

Benefits for singles

- By forging friendships with families, you can gain
  a sense of belonging unlike what you can experience with a single friend. This is especially wonderful if you have no family members nearby.

- If you have no children, you can gain immeasur-
  ably from involvement with your friends' children.

The value of this increases in importance as we age and our hopes of having our own children dim. Perhaps this is one of the ways in which the prophecy in Isaiah 54:1 is fulfilled for singles: "'Shout for joy, O barren one, you who have borne no child; break forth into joyful shouting and cry aloud, you who have not travailed; for the sons of the desolate one will be more numerous than the sons of the married woman,' says the LORD." This is a very comforting thought.

- Being this close to a couple and their children develops realism about marriage. It can provide firsthand, real-life training in marriage and raising children.

- You can derive a great sense of worth from friendships with families. When I feel an entire family wants me to be involved in their lives, this really builds me up! This can powerfully counter negative images we often feel we are fighting— things that easily work against a healthy self-esteem. For example, it is special to be included in holiday celebrations and family vacations.

- Friendships with families also broaden your opportunities for social events and recreational activities. Bridging the gap doubles your opportunities for socializing because you are no longer distanced from the half of the population that is married!

- It also is nice to have a family with whom to share everyday meals periodically. You can share meals with other single friends, but it's just different sitting around the family table. Conversely, when I invite families over to my house, it brings "life" to my home.

- If you are a single parent, close friendships with other families can foster healing, and their love can be like a refuge from the storm. Families can provide another avenue of interaction for your children.

- You have the opportunity to strengthen the marriages of close friends by giving practical support, prayer support and by helping them in the hard work of child raising.

- Being welcomed into a family circle goes a long way in helping you feel you "fit in" and are not an anomaly. For example, because of the up-close exposure I've had with families, I can relate so much better when I'm in a group of married people who are sharing stories of their family experiences. I'm a participant in the conversation instead of a bystander because I too understand the nature of their experiences.

- Friendships with couples also allow for refreshing, safe, "no-pressure" experiences with the opposite sex. When I'm not dating, and since I don't live near my brothers, friendships with families allow a wonderful opportunity for this dry area of my life to be watered. And it's really nice to feel like I have some "brothers" around—men who are looking out for me and with whom I can enjoy consistent fellowship. Single men also benefit in different ways by having some "sisters" around.

- There is great potential for awesome matchmaking when more couples interact with singles and can help bring us together. Inherent safeguards are included when you are introduced to someone who is known by friends you trust. Also, because the introducing couple knows the personalities and interests of both singles, there is more potential for higher success in striking a good match. *If there were more relationships across*

marital lines like this, there'd be more potential to
meet other singles in a comfortable, natural setting!

Several years ago, some married friends who knew me well knew of a man they thought would be a great match for me. The way we met was very comfortable because they arranged a way for him to meet me without my knowing what was up. There was no awkwardness and no pressure on either of us. We did date, and I believe we got off to a grand start largely because of the relaxed and natural way in which we met.

If you meet someone through a common connection with a couple, it is quite possible that that couple can form a mentoring relationship with you that can be very helpful as you date and also if you and the person to whom they introduced you should marry. The couple who introduced me to the man I mentioned above was invaluable to us as we dated and ultimately concluded not to marry.

In today's society, many of us do not live near our parents, siblings or other relatives. If we have no family of our own, and no relatives live nearby, how are we to experience any semblance of family life? Many of us try to address our own lack of family only by trying or hoping or wishing or praying to get married. But despite all the efforts and prayers, there are a lot of us who marry much later in life than we had hoped, and some who never marry. Meanwhile the clock ticks, and a lot of life can go by without experiencing any sense of family life. I'm forty-five. Had I not had the connections with families that I've had, I could have spent the last twenty-five years just looking for, *but never experiencing family*. Keep hoping and praying for your own family, yes, but meanwhile, you can be a lot happier and more satisfied if you enjoy the families you befriend.

Benefits for couples

- Friendships with singles provide an opportunity for couples to have well-rounded friendship circles. Many of our experiences are unique to couples.

These types of relationships broaden them and give them fresh perspectives. Couples have the opportunity to demonstrate Jesus' inclusive kind of love and purposefully extend themselves outside the "comfort zone" of their immediate family.

- You can be an additional strong Christian role model for your friends' children and can reinforce the values of their parents, which they greatly appreciate! This can be particularly beneficial if extended families are not close physically (or emotionally) and if you become a surrogate aunt or uncle to the children.

- A major thing couples can gain is extra help, especially in areas where you are gifted. If you have a great attitude and a big heart, you can chip right in and be "part of the family" in this way, too. This is particularly applicable to parents of babies and toddlers.

- Those of us without children may be able to provide assistance in emergencies or when unexpected needs arise. We often are more readily available to drop and go because we don't have to line up a babysitter or figure out a way to bring two or three children with us before we can rush to someone's aid.

- The potential exists for a deep love to be expressed for a friend's children by a childless single. Not having our own children, we can have a truly big heart to love and appreciate someone else's children.

- You can give couples time together by caring for their children while they enjoy a much needed "date night." They enjoy the added benefit of knowing that their children are in your hands instead of a young hired teenager.

If singles and couples were generally relating to each other in the ways I just described, we all would better understand the types of challenges each other faces and be more sensitive to each other. When couples better understand our needs and are convinced that our needs are valid, they are motivated to reach out and welcome us with open arms. I've watched God place compassion in the hearts of some couples after learning more about these things, where formerly they were just perplexed at why some singles seemed to struggle so. Couples are blessed by singles as they find the treasures God has for them in these types of relationships.

After seeing the benefits of these friendships, the next step is to overcome the separation factors currently hindering them from developing. Sometimes things that look like mountains are actually only molehills. Some things actually are mountains, but God can move mountains, and I've seen Him do it. So let's dig in and explore some solutions.

OVERCOMING COMMON SEPARATION FACTORS SINGLES FACE

The "pain of reminders"

You have to come to the place where you believe that what you have to gain is worth the pain that sometimes will accompany these friendships. I wish I could tell you those aches go away, but in my experience, they don't. I give it to Jesus as it is happening, and again afterward if my mind wanders back to it. Jesus bore our pain and suffering on the cross (Isa. 53:4). I take Him at His Word and make this a reality. Through prayer, I give Him the pain, and He gives me His resurrection power to go through it (Rom. 6:5). Jesus gives us the grace to manage our feelings so that this separation factor does not forever prevent us from experiencing all the benefits of having friendships with families.

Feeling like a "third wheel"

This can be overcome, but it takes understanding. Either you have to accept the situation and be very confident and self-assured, or the couple has to be sensitive to how you can feel like a misfit in these situations, thus working toward helping you feel genuinely included and wanted. It is better still when both you and the couple implement these strategies. But if you are weak in this regard, or if the couple is weak in this regard, still, the problem can be overcome by the one who is strong in dealing with this separation factor.

Feeling unwanted by a family

I believe that this, by and large, is purely a misconception we hold that has little basis in reality. Most often, I believe the truth really falls more along the line that a family simply hasn't thought about including a single because family-based friendships haven't been common. As the concepts discussed here become more widely known and understood, I believe this separation factor will fall away. Meanwhile, we can address this the same way we deal with the "third wheel" issue.

Don't see why it's good to have married friends

Hopefully the things I've discussed have helped you see why it's good. But there's nothing like experience to really convince you. So just try it!

OVERCOMING COMMON SEPARATION FACTORS COUPLES FACE

Viewing themselves as just a "boring married couple"

Let couples know that their life is very appealing to you and that you view many things they do as far from "boring." Also explain that you do not view in a negative light even the things that are seemingly boring, because it's their *friendship* that matters. Tell them you think that watching a video at home on a Saturday night is fun with *friends*. If you treasure interaction and friendship with their children, tell them so and indicate a desire to spend time with their family, *including the children.* Help them understand that while they may perceive your life to be "exciting" in contrast to theirs, you too have many responsibilities. Explain that even though their life may feel chaotic, it is a welcome and life-giving change of pace to you.

May feel odd to invite a single

I believe this will diminish over time as the concepts we've discussed become more common. Encourage married friends to push through what may seem awkward at first. Explain that you would surely feel it to be inappropriate to invite yourself along, so unless they invite you, it won't happen. While this surely feels awkward to explain to a friend, you need to. If they feel awkward and you bring up the subject in a positive and uplifting manner, you'll ease their awkwardness.

Commitments and interests of children

Perhaps you would welcome the opportunity to attend children's functions because you view it as a tangible way to demonstrate support to and interest in the children. Explain this to a couple, and explain again that, with no invitation, you likely will never invite yourself. Again, it likely will feel awkward to say these kinds of things, but this kind of involvement strengthens your relationship with that family. It also opens opportunities for you to form new relationships with others you may routinely see at a repeating function. And who knows, perhaps you just might meet a future mate when these kinds of invitations become commonplace!

Social decisions based on children's friendships

If you develop good relationships with their children, the children generally will love having you come over. They see it as a time when they get some undivided attention from an adult. You may not know how to form these types of relationships with children. Ask their parents to help you learn good ways of interacting with their children. They'll love the fact that you care!

Lack of understanding of what singles face or uncertainty about how to help

Open up your life. As you are vulnerable, your married friend will feel more comfortable about being vulnerable, too. This is just the way friendships work. Over time, you'll both learn what the other needs and ways to be a blessing. Give it time, and be patient.

Being somewhat overwhelmed by the known needs

All of us at times need encouragement to believe that our lives can make a difference to others. Tell your married friends that they may be surprised how strong their impact can be, even in small things. Explain that what may feel to them like only a "drop in the bucket" may feel like a refreshing wave to you! In the body of Christ, I believe Satan tries to undermine the extension of support by making all of us feel that our offering is too small. All of us have to push past this. So remind your friends (as you remind yourself) to give God a chance to multiply the effect of what they offer, as He did the loaves and the fish.

OVERCOMING COMMON SEPARATION FACTORS EXPERIENCED BY BOTH COUPLES AND SINGLES

Lack of common interests and lifestyle

Focus more on what you do have in common than what you don't share (for example, common interests in sports, creative arts, recreational pursuits, areas of serving in the church). With respect to differences, try to have an open attitude of expecting to learn new things from someone who holds different life experiences than you.

"This is just the way it is."

As Christians, there are many things in life that require us to go "against the grain" of society. This is just another area. God's ways are best. Remind yourself that you are honoring God as you carve new ways of relating, thereby bringing increased unity to the body of Christ. Accept the challenge of forging ahead into new territory. It's never been easy to be a pioneer. Those who forge the path make it easier for those who come after them. Go into it knowing it can be challenging and with a willingness to learn how to overcome the obstacles. Then enjoy the fruit of your labor as God blesses His work through you.

Envy

There are advantages and disadvantages both to being single and being married. We need to accept the disadvantages our lifestyle holds in contrast to someone else's. God always uses challenges and trials to mature us. Our trials often enable us to be a blessing to others who face similar trials. We need to rejoice genuinely for the advantages enjoyed by the person we are tempted to envy. (That is a sure way to overcome envy!) We need to focus attention on the blessings God has bestowed on us and express our thanks to Him and to others who enrich our lives.

Boundary issues: dependency, being "used," family identity distinctions

These three issues all come under the broader heading of knowing and maintaining appropriate boundaries in relationships. If a person has a problem relative to boundaries, it will be woven through all his or her relationships to one degree or another. It is not unique to just the relationship between singles and couples. However, God may use a relationship between a single and a couple to call attention to a boundary issue. These problems must be addressed at the root.

Ideally, it is best when both you and the couple know how

to establish and maintain healthy boundaries. If you don't start out that way, you either will learn, or the friendship ultimately won't work. While relationships between couples and singles have the potential to pose somewhat bigger boundary challenges than other types of friendships, honest and clear communication with the couple is the best remedy for working through any issues that arise. Boundary problems need not be insurmountable obstacles in forming and keeping family-based friendships. It is not possible to address all potential boundary issues, but all of the books on the subject of boundaries written by Dr. John Townsend and Dr. Henry Cloud are great resources for learning how to overcome the boundary issues that are common in life.[1]

Insecure about parenting skills

No matter how wonderful a relationship is between a single and a friend's child, the relational tie to a parent will not be surpassed. But if your friend is insecure, you need to talk this over to determine the best course of action. Again, God may be using this as an opportunity to shine His light on a problem area in order to bring new freedom. This should not be an insurmountable separation factor, but if the insecurity causes serious problems, it is time to reconsider the form of the friendship and whether significant adjustments should be made.

Acceptance by extended family members

There is potential for misunderstanding, even jealousy, of these types of friendships, on the part of yours or your friend's extended family members. It is best to have open and honest communication with extended family members regarding your motivation for pursuing family-based friendships and the value you derive from them. These friendships don't decrease the importance of our biological families or take their place. Extended family members will likely become very supportive once they understand the nature of the friendship.

Threat to marriage

No family-based friendship should ever threaten a marriage. Some couples might automatically discount a friendship with you due to fears about this issue. If the couple is insecure, they should not engage in family-based friendships (mountain-sized obstacle) and should instead give more attention to strengthening their marriage. If, however, the generalized fear is based only on misconceptions, those can be dealt with (molehill in reality). Some singles *assume* that the spouse of the same sex will automatically be jealous of any friendship with the family. As purely an *assumption*, this is unwarranted.

With rare exceptions, every family-based friendship needs to spring from a friendship that develops with a spouse who is of the same sex as the single friend. Those of the same sex should form the "primary friendship," which is a bridge to friendships with the rest of the family. The primary friendship between those of the same sex should be the strongest link in the chain. In those rare instances when a friendship does originate between a single and a spouse of the opposite sex, the same sex spouse must quickly become at least equally as bonded in friendship or the friendship should not continue, in my opinion. I don't advocate family-based friendships in which a friendship between a single and a spouse of the opposite sex is stronger than the friendship between those of the same sex.

You need to use common sense in this. If you are a person of character, you will make the right decisions and choices so that this issue is not even on the radar screen. I've had strong friendships with many couples over the last twenty-five years, and this issue has never arisen in any of those friendships. It certainly need not be an issue. Tragically, people commit adultery. It is committed not only between married and single persons, but also between two married persons as well. The character of those involved is much more the issue than whether a person is married or single. The dreadful fact that some people commit adultery should not, of itself, be a barrier that forever separates married people from singles.

PUTTING IT INTO PRACTICE

Now that you know many of the benefits of these friendships, recognize the obstacles and have a starting place for overcoming those obstacles, you may be ready to go. But you may be thinking, *OK, but how in the world do I actually do this? Where do I start?* Essentially, the tools we use in friendships generally are the same tools we use in building bridges with couples. There are, however, some special things to keep in mind, which call for adjustments in your approach. When it's all said and done, it comes down to three things: communication, understanding and doing things together.

Because of the differences between singles and couples, it is certain that misconceptions will arise. So expect them. The only way to clear up misconceptions is to explain your perspective—and sometimes re-explain it and re-explain it. There have been lots of points I've had to re-explain to my married friends and, likewise, they to me. It may be *hard* to communicate, but we *must* do it.

To build a healthy friendship, there has to be understanding on both sides of the relationship. We have to know and respect certain key things about the other person. We have to *act* on what we know. We also need to honor our friends and not criticize them if they do not intuitively understand certain things about us to the degree we wish they did.

Here's an example of challenging yet good communication that also depicts understanding. During those times when I get lonely no matter how hard I fight it, my closest friends and I agreed that I should always feel free to call them up and simply ask to come over. If it is not a good time for them, they *know* they can say *no* and that it is *really* OK. They know that I want a true and honest answer, because then I can trust them when they say *yes.* Consequently, when I've done the gutsy thing of swallowing my pride and inviting myself over, I don't have to second-guess or wonder whether it truly was OK that I came over. I can just relax and enjoy their company.

This kind of honesty has been hard, but it has been worth it. Being this honest has often felt unnatural. I *learned* how to be this honest; it wasn't automatic. I learned from practice and, yes, unfortunately, hard knocks. But it is good for all of us, married and single, to grow in learning how to sensitively explain our needs and desires.

A major building block of any relationship is time spent doing things together. For family-based friendships, this means activities both with your primary friend and with his or her family. Keep your primary friendship strong, but build a friendship with the family members, too. You can do this by recreating or working together. In my family-based friend-ships, we've skied together, painted houses together and just about everything in between.

Friendships between singles and families are as unique as friendships just generally are. Some will be very close, and others will be more peripheral. Some friends you may see or talk to several times a week or even daily. Others, you may get together with only once a month or so.

Differences in families greatly influence what a family-based friendship is like. For example, some families are very "open." Like a revolving door, they welcome everyone in and out. You'll find it's easier to feel included in this type of fam-ily. Other families are more "closed." They have a strong sense of identity and boundary, setting themselves apart from nonfamily members. While it may be difficult to feel accepted or included in a family like this, if you do become a part, it is very special.

Here's another helpful thing to keep in mind, which I offer by way of analogy. There are many things in life you head into that you didn't master beforehand. For example, often when you're promoted, you begin your new position wondering if you are really up for the task. You feel your way, learning as you go. So it is with these integrated friendships. Don't go into it thinking you *should* know how to do it. Also, give yourself and others room to make mistakes, learn and grow. Think well of your friend in terms of his or her ability to learn and change, and his or her desire to do so for the sake of the friendship.

It is possible to have great friendships across marital lines! Some of this may seem impossible or daunting, but it's not! I am living proof, as well as other singles I know. Having read this, you are in a good position to allow God to build faith in your heart for this work of His. Faith is a necessary component for moving forward in this. When the challenges come, those who have faith keep moving forward anyway. Remember the power of just one individual in the hands of God. God can do amazing things through those who are yielded to Him.

This is a win/win situation for both singles and couples. Although it should not be difficult to convince others of this, it simply is hard to change existing patterns. Consequently, the changes I'm suggesting will not happen overnight. But I do believe that change, even though it may come about slowly, *is* going to come. The shape and form of these changes will vary for each of us, as we are in different places and have different needs. Let's do what we can do, and be patient as God does what only He can do. By being integrated, we reflect to the world something uniquely precious about who God is and who we are as His people. God uses this to draw others in. The world is a lonely place for a lot of folks. We want to be an inviting place that has open arms.

Chapter 15

God Wove Our Lives Into a Beautiful Tapestry

One of the easiest ways to convey what I've written so far is to tell you our story—the story of four couples and me, and how God worked in our lives to reflect the beauty of Psalm 68:6: "God sets the solitary in families" (NKJV). Sometimes we never know the beauty of a scripture until it is lived out in front of us.

I moved to Columbus, Ohio, in the summer of 1989 and quickly became a member of Vineyard Church of Columbus. I was thirty-one and definitely concerned about my unmarried status. Hope springs eternal, though, and I hoped and prayed that somewhere in Columbus, God would lead me to a man I would love the rest of my life, and together we'd serve the Lord.

Shortly after moving to Columbus, I met Sue and Pat, who also had just moved here. Pat had just graduated from college, and Sue was starting law school. They were engaged and set to marry the following summer. They were very much in love, but their focus on each other didn't detract from their focus on others. They were warmhearted, and it was just their nature to love and serve those around them. Pat was an easy-going, totally likeable sort of a guy. Sue was passionate about everything important. Over the years I've learned that you can't plumb the depths of their compassion. We met at a home group, and that's how our friendship began. At that group, we also met Tim, who comes more into the picture a little down the road. He was in medical school and also had recently moved to Columbus for his residency.

Soon after that I met Terri at church. She was outgoing and vivacious and married to an affable guy named Rob. The two of them were quite a pair. They could easily draw in anybody. It wasn't hard to tell that Terri was the consummate evangelist! Bold, assured—a real truth-teller. She loved Jesus and wanted everyone else to also.

Summer ended, fall came and went, and in the heart of winter, I met Betsy. We also met at church by no small coincidence (that's a long story). She was a distributor for a nationwide shoe store chain. She took a leap of faith to move to Columbus, uprooting from all that was familiar in her home state of Kansas. We instantly hit it off, exchanging histories and laughing at each other's stories as we got to know one another. Betsy was really easy to talk to, and she had a smile that lit up the room. One thing I learned about Betsy early on was that she was loyal to the bone. She cared a lot about the people she loved. She was my link to Debbie.

It so happened that Betsy started attending the same women's Bible study that Terri led (not even knowing that Terri and I knew each other—God's providence at work). Debbie also attended that same group, and the three of them became friends. At a conference our church hosted in February, Betsy and Terri introduced me to Debbie, and we all decided to sit together. Well, you would have thought we'd all known each other for years already! We spent most of that conference weekend together. It was that weekend that God started weaving our lives into a beautiful tapestry, which later came to include their husbands, Sue and Pat, and all the children who followed.

One of the most obvious things I noticed about Debbie soon after meeting her was that she was tenderhearted and kind to everyone. Without even trying, she made everyone around her feel special and cared for. She'd do anything for anybody. The love of God radiated through her eyes, joy beamed through her smile, and she often had a spring in her step.

Of the five of us women, one was married, one engaged, one was dating and two were totally detached. Debbie was in love with a fun, smart guy getting his MBA at Arizona State, but since it was a long-distance relationship, she seemed about as "single" as Betsy and I were—for a while. It didn't take long for everything to change. Within a few months, Betsy caught Tim's eye, and the rest is history. (Did God have a plan for Betsy moving to Columbus, or what?) Mike, the smart guy in Arizona, knew what a treasure he had in Debbie, so as soon as he could pull out of Arizona State, he was on her doorstep with engagement on his mind. So my "carefree" single days with these women were short lived. It was in the spring that year (1990) that Betsy and Tim started dating, and they had a June wedding the following year. Sue and Pat nestled down that summer as planned. Debbie and Mike married in the spring of 1992. So where did this leave me?

This pattern was nothing new for me. By then I had already watched many friends get married all around me. (I began to wonder if I was wearing a sign that said, "Hey, don't even *think* about dating me!") So I already knew the drill on how friendships change after marriage. It was just a reality of life, and I accepted it. Yet, it was hard, because it had happened so many times by that point.

Although I wondered when it would be "my turn," my lack did not keep me from truly and fully rejoicing with them when they said *yes* to that all-important question. I screamed, I yelled, I cried. I rejoiced completely *for them* at their weddings. Sometimes I think people assume that because you are sad about your position, you cannot be happy for someone who is in the position you'd like to be in. It's not true. I *was* sad for myself, but that didn't prevent me from being genuinely happy for them. I *loved* them. I truly wanted them to be as happy as they could possibly be!

Now, this happy-sad thing was a pattern that repeated itself over and over again—when they each bought their first house, then second. When they each got pregnant, and then pregnant again, and again, and again. I entered into those occasions with them. I screamed, I yelled, I rejoiced when they told me they were pregnant. Terri was first to start the rounds. Sue was last. For a variety of reasons, there was a lot of praying that had to go into some of those pregnancies. I prayed for the babies before conception and after. I prayed for the moms during pregnancy and *especially* after! I helped put on the showers. I remember waiting, waiting, waiting for the phone to ring so that I could hear, "It's a boy!" and erupt in shouts of joy. I went to the hospital. I held the new babies. I stayed with child number one while child number two was born. I was right in there with them, all the way, no holds barred for, between all four of them, eleven babies! They were my *friends*. I loved them dearly. In no way did I despise the good gifts that God was pouring out. I prayed He would bless them abundantly.

But at the same time, my heart did break, at times, for myself. While this went on, though, I didn't have an issue with *them*. As time wore on, I later had an issue with God (which we'll get to), but never with them. That perspective just would have been all wrong. Surely they should receive everything God had for them! A husband or wife is a good gift (Prov. 18:22), and children are a blessing from the Lord (Ps. 127:3).

It's very important that you know I was not bitter about their blessings. This is such an important distinction because I'm trying to explain the way *a lot* of singles feel. But it gets confused. Some people assume we can't or won't rejoice for others. We can and do; it's just that *at the same time*, we might also naturally be hurting inside.

MY DWINDLING BORDERS

Before I continue with our story I have to explain more about the things I was experiencing. While all this was going on for them, the *exact opposite* was going on for me. Their borders were expanding, and mine were dwindling. You see, these

weren't my only friends. I had a lot of other friends, too—
many of them also still single. Yet one by one, many of those
friends got married, too. So here's the dynamic that began to
evolve: Increasingly I had fewer and fewer people to socialize
with because they were with their spouses. I became progres-
sively more despairing as Friday and Saturday nights
approached. And the strange thing was, I still had *really good*
friends, just fewer socializing opportunities.

More and more, people began directing me toward singles
events. I tried going to lots of different kinds of singles functions hosted by various churches. This, however, did not
resolve things for me. But since none of the people recom-
mending I attend such functions had ever been to any, they
couldn't understand why I did not want to go. They sometimes interpreted this as my "not trying hard enough" or my
unwillingness to "get out there," although this wasn't true.

I was very active in my church. I was highly involved in
evangelism, discipleship, women's ministry, my home group
and in our church's peer counseling ministry. I had no problem filling my time. Just keeping my personal life in order was
very challenging. So when I say I was active, that is not the
same as saying I was fulfilled and satisfied relationally. There's
a difference between serving and recreating. We all need some
time to just kick back, be with friends and get refreshed.

Despite the fact that I was very active and had many friends
through these various ministry connections, I was still very
lonely. To look at me externally, I'm sure most church leaders
assumed I had a busy social calendar. But the fact of the matter was, I didn't. Interestingly, at a party I attended, one of my
pastors told me that I was one of the most "connected" people
he knew. Yet with all these good, strong friendships, I often
would find myself alone. My phone didn't ring much other
than for periodic calls received from my closest friends and, of
course, telemarketers. Literally, days would go by with not
one personal call…not even a message. I was baffled.

I knew in my heart of hearts that I was very loved, yet I had such a barren social life. I wondered, *What is wrong with this picture?* Here I was, a normal, healthy, fun-loving, Christian woman. I should be "alive" on the weekends, just like the world around me. While it seemed most others looked forward to the weekends, I dreaded them. It just was so strange. I felt normal, yet my life seemed so abnormal compared to those around me.

So you see, it wasn't just that friends were getting married, and I wasn't, or that friends were having babies, and I wasn't. That was hard enough. But it was exponentially compounded by the fact that, increasingly, my social life was withering up. In my earlier days in high school and college, I was incredibly active. So I thought this was going to drive me crazy. Formerly I had been very much an "out there" kind of person. I was used to leading the charge and being in the middle of all the action. I loved being with people. I loved being on the go. I loved almost every imaginable kind of recreational activity. Everything about me screamed that I was born to be with people. And what was I facing? A life that was going in the exact opposite direction, and it was totally out of my control.

I know you might be thinking to yourself, *Oh, well, I see what God was up to—He was taking you into a serious refining time.* I agree, because it sure has been. But please understand that it is hard to comprehend what in the world is going on when you feel as if you are being forced to become a totally different person than you actually are. This is especially hard to comprehend at the time you are going through it. It doesn't make sense.

I'd pray, "God, You *made* me this way. *You* did. Why would You be turning me into something totally opposite? I like being me. I hate this other thing it seems I'm becoming. I don't want to be a loner. I don't want to sit at home. I hate isolation. Please don't make me go down this path." All the while I was also desperately trying to keep praying, "... but Thy will be done...*Thy* will, not mine."

Another thing making this really hard was that I just couldn't see any purpose behind it at all. It's one thing to "go to the cross" because you know somebody will be saved through it—but I couldn't see any benefit in this. Being the "real" me, I felt vibrant and useful. I was a blessing to others. And I was close to God. But this other person I was becoming was just so contrary to all that I thought I was. Instead of being a blessing, I felt I was becoming a burden. And I felt I was drifting farther from God when I would find myself saying, "My God, my God, why have You forsaken me?"

And how do you explain this to others? How do you explain it to your closest friends, especially when their lives are going in the opposite direction? Here they were living out their dreams, while one by one, my dreams were falling away to nothingness—just gone—lost forever. No hope of my own children. No hope of grandchildren. No hope of their graduations and weddings and everything in between. It's just gone. From my perspective, my friends were on the mountaintop, even with the dirty diapers and the screaming that lasted for hours (yes, even that), because they have an absolutely priceless treasure in every child. And God willing, when the children are out from under the roof, they will still have a loving husband. Through all their trials and all the heartaches, with even more that I knew were sure to come, I still viewed them as being on the mountaintop.

How can somebody on the mountaintop commune with somebody in the valley? There's only one thing that can span that distance, and it's love. It is because of God's love for us and our love for one another that we've been able to maintain our relationships with one another though our lives are very different. And different not just because they're married and I'm single, but as you hopefully can see more clearly now, because we're in dramatically different spots in another realm as well— one that can't be seen and that is hard even to describe.

So that is the backdrop against which the rest of this story should be viewed. You can see there is room for a lot of turmoil and tumult, but through it all, God kept winning, because "love never fails." It "bears all things, believes all things, hopes all things, endures all things." (See 1 Corinthians 13.) By God's grace, that's what we have continued to do. We've stumbled. We've fallen—sometimes hard. But we've gotten back up and kept on going. As I said, Betsy's loyal to the bone. Sue's compassion knows *no* end. Debbie will do anything for you, and I mean *anything*, including entering into your "hell" with you when necessary. And Terri stands up for truth, even when people don't want to hear it.

A FRIEND LOVES AT ALL TIMES

We're all very different—in some respects, as different as night and day. And that also has caused us problems, as it does in all relationships. God uses us to refine one another. "Iron sharpens iron, so one man sharpens another" (Prov. 27:17). But the same beloved Book of Proverbs also says, "A friend loves at all times" (Prov. 17:17).

So why did we stay friends after they married, anyway? Well, the bottom line is that we *wanted* to. The fact that our lives were growing increasingly more different didn't overcome our desire to remain friends. It was worth it to us to work out the differences (even though *sometimes*, that value *did* seem a little uncertain). So we did. Some friends come and go in your life, but these are the kind that stay forever.

Our friendships had to evolve through the various changes that took place as each of these families changed. When the husbands came, that was an adjustment. Priorities for Sue, Betsy and Debbie changed, and there was less time and energy for their friendships with me. They (plus Terri) could relate to each other in ways I couldn't since I didn't share their common experiences. My self-esteem started taking a hit in a way that probably doesn't seem intuitively obvious. Always in the past, I could ask these women if they wanted to go and do something, and I felt that my opinions and desires were important enough to be taken into consideration. But now, much of the time it wasn't just the "girls" getting together. It was two or three or all four couples and me. When it came to making plans, I always felt as if I just had to defer to them because my opinion didn't count much. There was always at least one pair and then just me. To me, the opinion of a pair or two, or especially three, always felt far more weighty than any opinion I might have. So I just went along. At first, I didn't know why I felt "puny" when discussing plans. Gradually, though, I realized this repeating pattern.

I remember talking with Betsy on the phone one day, and I had a revelation of why I was feeling the way I did in the midst of one of our planning discussions. So we talked about it. I explained how I felt and why. She understood, and by uncovering that, we gained new understanding of one another and our different situations. Nothing revolutionary changed after that in terms of what we *did* about it, but a lot changed in terms of how I felt. After that conversation, I knew that Betsy would be aware of what this generated in me, and I knew I needed to work on not caving in to low self-esteem over it. I had to conscientiously remind myself that I was important and my opinion did count, and I always should feel free to express it. Betsy and the others learned that sometimes they might have to make an extra effort to ask my opinion just to make it a little easier on me.

I realized I had to explain this to other important couples in my life. That was hard. I remember explaining this to my sister, who is married with two children. She was *so willing*, however, to make extra efforts to include me in decision-making once she understood this! This was particularly helpful when it came to holiday plans. Prior to that, I always felt that I just "came into" whatever holiday my sister or brother planned, but had no say-so in it. I felt less a part of it—more like an outsider coming in, than a family member who's on the "inside" helping to make it happen. Although it was very hard to be this honest and vulnerable, it was so worth it. This one little understanding revolutionized my relating with couples and families from that time on. "You shall know the truth, and the truth shall make you free" (John 8:32).

A similar but different problem that I had to tackle was feeling like a third wheel when several of these couples got together. One year, Betsy and Tim, Terri and Rob, Debbie and Mike and I got together for New Year's Day. I wanted to share that holiday with them, but when we actually got together, my spirit sank. I didn't want to be in a funk, but I couldn't snap out of it. There they were, three "units"—and then there was me. Talk about a fish out of water. *What am I doing here?* I thought.

Yet here were these dear friends whom I loved and who loved me. I didn't want to spoil their day, so I put on the *happy face*. But they saw through it. As you can imagine, the whole thing just wasn't easy or pretty. Frankly, there was hurt, some resentment and lots of misunderstanding. They didn't know what it felt like to be in my shoes. To a certain degree, there was even a little resistance to want to understand it. Feeling that resistance initially made me less willing to open up in the future. That bothered me, because I knew that friendships suffer when you stop believing you can be honest with one another.

Well, that's where God came in! He softened hearts, gave grace and got us to the other side of it. We worked through it and prayed for one another. They understood better how I could feel so out of place, and I, in turn, had to work at relating to all of them as individual friends, not *pairs*. I also had to work on believing that I really did "belong" in that setting. I belonged because of my relationships. I didn't *not* belong because I was different—because I was single.

I also had to work at resisting the power of the ingrained

negative image of the stereotypical single. Viewing myself through the lens of this stereotype made me feel inferior just because I was single. It was easy to put myself "below" married people. I did this *unconsciously*, and I believe many singles do so also. This inferior feeling is a big component that fuels the third-wheel mentality. I had to make a quality decision to fight that.

The hard lesson learned in this context carried over to all my other relationships with couples. Let's take my home group, for example. I can walk into the living room and see ten couples, one other single and me, or I can see twenty-one *people* and me. In other words, I see Craig and Linda, not *CraigandLinda*. I see Ron and Nancy, not *RonandNancy*. It's not that I don't view these folks as *married*, which obviously is an important distinction. But we can choose the aspect of a person upon which we focus. Are we going to view them as *individuals* with whom we are free to have a healthy relationship, or as corporate *"couples"* who exist on a different plane than us and with whom we can't relate? Will we choose to base our belonging on *relationships* or marital status? Will we see ourselves with the stereotype filter over our eyes, or for who we truly are? The choice is ours. It can be hard to start relating according to these guidelines rather than old mindsets, but I can attest that it does get easier.

WHEN CHILDREN ENTER THE PICTURE

When the children started coming, there were brand-new things I had to learn how to overcome. Terri quit her job and had her first child; then Betsy, then Debbie, then Sue. And then they all went on to round two. Debbie and Betsy went on to round three. And Betsy, God bless her, went on to round four! With each child, I knew there'd be less and less time and energy these friends would have for me. Our recreational opportunities decreased dramatically. It's similar to what we experienced when the men entered their lives, but markedly increased. Priorities changed even more. Children brought an entirely new dimension to everything.

I knew I was facing the loss of increasing amounts of their time, and with that came decreasing recreational opportunities. Now they all shared another thing in common to which I did not relate experientially. Plus, all of them were stay-at-home moms, so we didn't even have the career side of our lives in common. It is all too easy in this situation to begin thinking, *What in the world do I have to offer you? Nothing.* And talk about feeling outnumbered and overshadowed! *Where do I fit into this picture? Nowhere!* Wrong. Thank God, that was and is the wrong answer. I had a lot to offer these friends and their little ones. But at first I couldn't see that. Something was blocking my view.

One of the hardest lessons for me to learn has been how to overcome what you've heard me refer to as the "pain of reminders." It didn't come together for me all at once, though; God took me through an important process. I used to find that two different things were going on in me at once. Part of me really wanted to be with these friends and their families, and another part of me wanted to run away as fast and as far as I could. The thing that drew me was that I really loved these friends, so naturally I wanted to share experiences with them. But the thing that made me want to run away was that being with them served as a *constant* reminder to me of what I didn't have: a husband, children and a seemingly endless social circle. There was a tug-of-war, and sometimes a raging battle, going on inside me.

God had taught me something early on, however, when my friends first started getting married. He showed me that I could view the husbands as new friends automatically added to my life, or I could view them as detractors who made it more difficult to continue friendships. Guess which one I chose? "I have set before you *life* and *death*, the blessing and the curse.

So *choose* life in order that you may live..." (Deut. 30:19, emphasis added). Because I loved these four women so much, I chose to love those whom they loved. Having learned this during the marrying stage, I applied it to the childbearing stage. I wanted to view these precious children as little disciples I could help my friends raise and lead to Jesus. I didn't want to view them as inconveniences or selfishly view them as the ones stealing things like my recreational pursuits.

I watched these mothers intently, trying to learn all I could. I changed diapers, learned all kinds of things about feeding and tried to calm the babies when they cried (and consoled my friends when their babies wouldn't stop crying). Well, children have a way of getting into your heart, don't they? Bonds formed.

The aches continued too, though. I'd watch Luke, Betsy's oldest, run toward her with reckless abandon when she entered the room. I'd watch Debbie make the world seem right in Ben's eyes just by lovingly placing a Band-Aid on his knee. There were countless opportunities each time I was with them to focus on what they had that I wanted so much. An interesting thing was happening, however. *Sometimes,* Luke or Ben *would* genuinely be excited to see *me.*

Regardless of the bonds, at times it seemed too hard. I was praying so earnestly that God would bless me with a spouse, and *quickly*! But if He wasn't going to do that, then at least give me new friends just as close as these—but *single*. I actually used to express great consternation and frustration to God that He continued to strengthen and bless these friendships, yet not give me new *single* friends. I'm sad to admit that there were times I caved in to thinking God was being cruel. I used to utter holy laments as David did in the Psalms, only mine went something like this: "You won't give me a husband, and You have all my closest friends get married. It's like You want to torture me. Why are You doing this?" I did not see the big picture God had in store down the road. Sometimes He hems us in and gives us nowhere else to go. I couldn't leave Him, and I couldn't leave these friends. If you're not going to leave God or your friends, and you can't change your situation, eventually you start resigning yourself to God's plan. God began to show me that there was so much more to be gained by resisting the temptation to run. He challenged me to bite the bullet and sometimes endure the pain that comes with the reminders. I have a choice. When I see my friend and her husband snuggled on the couch, I can either rejoice over the strength of their marriage, or I can dwell on the fact that I'm sitting in a chair by myself. Or when Laura, Debbie's three-year-old, comes rushing into my arms, I can either cherish that experience as being totally precious for what it is, or I can bemoan the fact that it isn't *my* three-year-old rushing into my arms.

I can remember a day as God was teaching me this—it is so clear in my mind. I was playing with Debbie's two little boys— Ben and Zach—in my backyard. We were having a grand old time. I loved every minute—watching them excitedly run through my sprinkler...hearing their squeals of delight... observing the simplicity of their joy in small things.

I was sitting in a chair under my tree, and God gently dropped this thought into my heart, *You know, you almost missed this.* And just as it often is when God gives you a revelation, you know instantly what He meant. In one brief thought He conveyed to me the power of my choices. Had I decided to cling to the path of protecting myself from the pain of reminders, and had I refused to look at things in a new way, I'd have missed out on what is absolutely priceless. The perspective I decide to take makes all the difference. And it is my choice to make, and mine alone. More and more, as I have made good choices, God has opened up the door for me to richly enjoy all the benefits of these family-based friendships. There is no more tug-of-war. Instead of running away from them, I now run to these families.

Is it still hard to face the pain of reminders? At times, yes.

The reminders will *always* be there. My desires will always be there. There's no getting away from that. I know there will be days and instances where I'll observe something, and it just *will* hurt. But I'm willing to endure it. There are elements of pain in all relationships. However, God has woven me into their lives, and them into mine, and the love that binds us is stronger than the pain that otherwise would separate us.

One of the hurdles the gang had to jump for us to get to this place was believing that I *wanted* to spend time with their children. They remembered younger single days when, yes, frankly, we all kind of did look at being around children as an inconvenience. And now as parents, although they love the children of their friends, they are not seeking opportunities to spend time with them. Plus, no one knows their children better than they do. They see the difficulties and challenges their children sometimes present. So, it was hard for them to grasp my genuine desire to play with, love and invest in their children.

I had to tell them over and over that I really *wanted* to play with their children. They thought I was "just being nice." They thought I was doing it *only* to give them some "down" time. But the idea that I actually *wanted* time with Luke, Ellie, Ben and Meredith, for example—well, that was a foreign concept. When I told Debbie what God had revealed to me in my backyard while watching Ben and Zach, she was deeply touched, yet it still was hard to take this in at first. Over time, though, it's become more than believable to them—it's become a happy reality.

TRAIL BLAZING

There are many other things we had to learn to get to this place. For example, these friends knew how much I wanted to be married and have children, so we learned how to tackle things like, how did they share their joy with me over new milestones in the lives of their children? How could they sensitively express elation over other wonderful family events,

knowing all the while that I was without? In other words, how
did they share what to them were natural joys that they knew
to me could spark personal heartache? Likewise, I needed to
address things like how do I express genuine joy over their
good news when inside my own heart is wrenching? How do
I support them when they are struggling with things I have
absolutely no experience in?

We've crossed those bridges and many more. I've given you
only a few examples out of many where we encountered
issues, and, through *a process* of making choices to be honest
and vulnerable and stick with each other, we worked things
out. We've learned and grown, and all of us are better off for
it. I am extremely thankful that my relationships with these
four women didn't just drop off as some others have after marriage. They remained strong; although, naturally, they did
change. We carved this path, but only recently have we had
God's insight to look back and see what He was doing all
along, to see the beautiful picture He was creating while we
were unaware.

It wasn't intuitively obvious to any of us that God wanted it
to work this way. Why? Because none of us had any exposure
to other families we knew who had really good, family-like
friendships with singles. As I look back over what we've experienced, I realize that we were blazing a trail without benefit-
ing from the experience of anyone we knew who'd gone
before us. Nobody gave us a road map and said, "Here—here's
how a single person maintains a friendship with a married
couple with children." We cut our teeth learning how to
remain friends though our lives were very different. That's
why we'd like to spare others from having to learn the hard
way. We hope our testimony makes things easier for those
who hear it.

So what difference does all this make to me now? After
more than twelve years of friendship together, where are we?
Well, I feel acceptance and warmth and belonging in a way I

did not before these relationships evolved to where they are today. I feel that I have a bunch of nieces and nephews right here in town. And now I get in on so many of the things I formerly couldn't enjoy, like going to the fair or the zoo or some other family outing *with children*. I share meals at their tables. I take their children to the park or have them over to my house. I read them bedtime stories and talk to them about Jesus.

The children give me hugs and smiles, and sometimes they let me dry their tears. Though I don't have children of my own to teach and watch grow and experience all the milestones with, I can enter into that through these genuine connections with my friends' children. I sometimes sit and think about what it will be like to attend their graduations and weddings (hopefully!). I look forward to being a part of the important events in their lives.

WHEN CHILDREN SHOWER YOU WITH LOVE

Oh, my, the love that I feel for these little boys and girls is amazing. I never imagined it could be this way. I love to think of what I can sow into their lives through time, attention and, most importantly, love. I believe I am going to make a difference in their lives. I cannot adequately describe what these children give to me, but I think you can grasp it when I explain some of our interactions and the memories they've already dropped into my soul. So you'll know who's who as I describe these events, here are the family connections: Debbie and Mike's children are Ben, Zach and Laura; Sue and Pat's children are Jonathan and Sam; Betsy and Tim's children are Luke, Ellie, Ben and Meredith; Terri and Rob's children are Austin and Cody. Here is a *small* sampling of the joys they've given me:

I got to be in the delivery room when Meredith entered this world! I also was warmly welcomed to be present at Jonathan's delivery, and would have had I been able.

One evening when I had dinner at Betsy's, Ellie gave the prayer of thanks for our meal. She ended with, "And thank You, God, that Virginia could be with us today." When this comes unprovoked and from the heart, what a treasure it is to hear these words.

Every time I see Cody, he always says, "It's nice to see you. How was your day?" He looks me in the face with his sweet blue eyes sparkling and his tender smile, and he really *wants* to know!

Betsy's Ben turned the tables on me recently when he nestled by my side and wanted to read to *me*! (He's only five!) And I hope I never forget the time he complimented me on one of my prayers for him.

One day I came home from work to a message from Jonathan. Can you imagine how it feels to have a four-year-old call to thank you for his birthday presents, tell you how much he likes them and close with, "I 'yuv' you"?

Recently as I've worked on the book, I haven't seen any of the children very much. The other day, Laura wrapped herself around my leg and told me she *really* missed me. (Makes you want to cry!)

I had to choke back the tears the day Zach asked me if he and I could get married when he was older.

When I visit Betsy's, Meredith usually comes *running* to the door to greet me! Recently when the gang of us watched fireworks on the Fourth of July, Meredith wanted to sit next to me. Without fail, after every display, she'd look up at me with the broadest smile and twinkling eyes and tell me how much she liked "that one." She was so happy to share her joy with me, and she was intent on knowing my reaction, too.

I remember a special day at church when Luke told me he'd given his heart to Jesus—the day every Christian parent longs for. I was so blessed that he wanted to share that priceless announcement with me, too. I have another special memory of Luke at church. He was part of a worship song and routine that the children did. I remember tearing up to see him on stage. It was then that I realized I had finally grasped what I call "the kid thing." It didn't used to pull on my heartstrings when children were involved in special worship songs at church. I knew it did for the parents, but not for me. Well, I finally got it. I now understand "the kid thing."

I've also had the great pleasure of spending two Christmas holidays with Sue and Pat and their boys, who now live in Colorado. It is a joy to be there on Christmas morning and watch Jonathan and Sam delight in their gifts! They also delight in giving gifts to me! My stocking is hung right alongside theirs. We carry on traditions started when they lived in Columbus, like all-day Christmas-cookie baking.

Debbie's family gave me the time of my life when they included me on a five-day, fun-filled family vacation last summer! We've also taken many weekend camping trips together.

I've been present when almost all of the children were dedicated. I watched Austin be baptized and shared in the family celebration afterwards.

You know you're like one of the family when you're in on a family photo. Last year I was taking the holiday photo for Debbie's family, and suddenly, Zach said, "You get in the picture too, Ms. Virginia!" I was also really touched when Sue and Pat wanted me to have a professional photo done with their family. They placed me squarely in the middle, depicting my belonging. These photos say it all. A picture is worth a thousand words.

I recall saying bedtime prayers one night with Ben and Zach, and it was precious to me when Ben asked God to "please bring Ms. Virginia a husband so she can have kids like us."

Nothing beats walking through Debbie's door and having Laura run into my arms, yelling, "Ms. Virginia! Ms. Virginia!"

Everyone's artwork has taken rotations on my refrigerator,

and their annual portraits are scattered throughout my house.

The last time I visited Sue's, Sam couldn't quite talk yet, but he says a million things with his eyes and smile, and he always showers me with love and affection. And even at his tender young age, he too has contributed some stunning artwork to my collection.

Are you getting the picture? Do you see why it's worth it to go through the pain of reminders? Can you understand why I'd wish for this to be duplicated countless times over throughout the body of Christ?

I don't mean to make this sound like a Hallmark commercial, because like everything in life, it still is a mixed bag at times. There continue to be some downsides, but clearly, the good far outweighs the bad. And I recognize this is a big piece of the solution God has provided for me. In this season of my life, as I have remained single in opposition to my most heartfelt desire, God has been true to His Word in Psalm 68:6 and has set me in a family—in fact, in several! God saw my pain, and He has soothed it tremendously through these family-based friendships. I don't feel so alone anymore—so "out there." I am single, but not separate. I believe that I have something priceless I can give to these families, and there is a place in their lives where I belong.

FAMILY TIES

I have to tell you that as these ties became stronger I worried what my family would think of me having these family-like friendships. Would they think I did not value my relationships with them as much? I didn't want to hurt them, but I have not lived in the same locale as any of my natural family members for over twenty-five years. Should I continue to deny the experience of having a sense of family nearby so as not to hurt them? Eventually, this was another thing I needed to address in a straightforward manner. I talked with them. Again, they did not know my perspective, having not walked in the shoes of a single. Once they did, they were so understanding. Now, they even ask about these friends in much the same way they would if they actually were family. By treating these friends that way, my family demonstrates to me a degree of support and love that I formerly had not experienced because I had not given it a chance to come out for fear of hurting them. Another lesson learned.

So, looking back, we all *know* we owe this all to God. But I have to say, beyond Him, I owe so much to these friends and their children. It was through them that God opened my eyes to many of the things that are at the heart of this book. They have been an inspiration to me in wanting to pass this along to others. While I have naturally focused much attention on the wives, I do pay special tribute to all the husbands for supporting these friendships. Had they not been so open and receptive, none of these things would have taken place. They are godly men. I know there are many more out there just like them who will welcome these types of friendships. And there are godly wives who will welcome their husbands' friends into their family circle as well.

BROADEN YOUR CIRCLE OF FRIENDSHIPS

These kinds of quality people are out there, and you needn't limit family-based friendships to only the families of friends you had while both friends were still single. This wasn't the case with Terri, nor has it been the case for me with many other wonderful couples whose friendships I hold very dear. I focused on the story of these four couples and me because our experiences depict so many of the unique challenges that singles and couples must maneuver through and overcome in creating and maintaining family-based friendships, especially as they evolve. But my friendship circle with couples is much broader than this. And it results not just from *my* efforts to reach out to couples, but also from *their* efforts to reach out to me.

Phil and Judy, my home group leaders, are a great example of a couple who know how to pull singles into their social circle. It is natural for them. They simply view me and other singles in our group as *people* they love, not as "singles." It doesn't seem that they even give a second thought about whether we are single or married when it comes to invitations. They love us, so they invite us. They've invited me to their parties, and out to eat, and on bike rides, and camping, and over to their house, and even out to Wyoming one summer! It feels good to be around them. I never feel like a third wheel. And all the singles I know feel the same way about Phil and Judy. We're welcome. We're a part, not set apart. I look at them and I think, *Now this is the way it's supposed to be. This is what God intended.* You see, it's one thing to welcome singles into a home group. But it's another to welcome them into your *social circle*. That's a whole different dimension. This is the type of relating we need to multiply in the church. As the saying goes, "More is caught than taught." Is it any wonder, then, that other couples in that home group relate to singles in much the same way? When it's modeled, people see it, and it becomes the new norm.

Craig and Linda, pastors at my church, also model this superbly. I first started to get to know Linda at church. I met her before I understood all I've been writing in this book. Because she was married, I kind of unconsciously discounted any notion of us becoming *good* friends. It was one thing to be friends with married women I knew before they married—and with Terri it was made easier because she was *part* of the "gang." It was something else to start a friendship with someone who *already* was married and with whom I did not have any specific social ties. But Linda reached out to me. She started inviting me to lunch periodically. Gradually I realized that we were actually becoming good friends. And then I got to know Craig and their children, too. They've invited me over for Thanksgiving and New Year's and Memorial Day, and even to the Outer Banks of North Carolina! Linda and Craig and their children welcomed me with open arms, and I am forever grateful. I've never felt like a third wheel around them either—not even in the beginning of our friendship. Why? Because I know there's not even a trace of that in their hearts toward me. It's nice that I don't even have to battle against the odd-man-out feeling. I'm a part, and it just doesn't matter at all that my part doesn't have a spouse attached.

Well, I could go on about other family-based friendships I enjoy, but the book would be too long. I hope I've given enough of a feel for this so that you can start writing your own stories. I pray that countless numbers of you in the body of Christ will reach across marital lines. Our heavenly Father will smile the biggest, proudest smile as He sees His children truly relating as "family"—blessing each other in ways He's always intended.

Every person makes a difference. Surely you see that there is a multiplication factor in all of this. As you can tell from these stories, we each carry what we learn into other friendships. We pass it on, and many benefit. By these experiences, we all are better able to relate across marital lines, which in turn is good for the body of Christ. So we should never underestimate the effect we can have as individuals, even when what we offer seems like only a drop in the bucket. One drop produces many ripples. And while we may not always see the impact of those ripples, God does—and every ripple matters to Him.

Chapter 16

Friends From the Christian Angle

Another primary avenue God has designed for meeting our relational needs is for us to live near friends. Warner Brothers' sitcom *Friends* begins each show with the words from its opening song: *"I'll be there for you…"* Those words convey a message we want to give and receive. We want to know that somebody is going to be there for us, and we take joy in assuring others that we will be there for them, too.

If you extract the casual sex and related innuendoes from *Friends*, in large part it describes what I mean when I say that our relational needs can be met to a great degree by living near enough to friends to give and receive support. Although people want these kinds of relationships, we don't see many in the real world today. The root elements driving this kind of lifestyle have slowly eroded from our culture. Much can be gained, however, if we encourage one another to rebuild this type of lifestyle back into the real world—into our world.

Before change can be successful, we must determine the root cause of the problem. What is it about our culture that makes it hard for singles to see this as a solution and pursue it? One challenging factor is the deeply seated individualism that permeates our heritage and current way of life. *Individualism* is defined as "belief in the primary importance of the individual and in the virtues of self-reliance and personal independence…the doctrine that the interests of the individual should take precedence over the interests of the state or social group."

Historically, individualism has been an admirable characteristic of our society. For example, it was evident in the founding era when our forefathers didn't want a strong central government usurping individual liberties. We can also observe it by reading about the lives of rugged frontiersmen and women who developed uncharted territories. But as our culture has drifted further and further away from Judeo-Christian principles, the individualism that was once rooted in self-sacrifice has increasingly become rooted in selfishness. Consequently, "community" breaks down, because community survives only in an environment of love, which is self-sacrificing instead of self-serving.

We see evidence of this in our neighborhoods. Front porches have turned into fenced backyards. People hardly know the person next door, let alone those on the entire block, as it was when I was growing up.

Additionally, many people today are reluctant to make commitments to a community of others. For example, when people become members at my church, our pastor acknowledges that making that type of commitment to a community has increasingly become more rare.

More evidence of this breakdown arises out of the attacks of September 11, 2001. Not until we were attacked was there much display of national unity. In addition, the corporate corruption we witnessed in 2002 further depicts focus on the individual at the expense of many others.

We also see the erosion of community in that there previously were more extended families who lived close by one another and who were knit into the social fabric of the larger community. Now families are spread all over, and there is a heightened sense of focus on just the nuclear family. This dwindling down to the smallest common denominator likely has a lot to do with the heightened divorce rate as the focus on the individual increases. The circle just keeps getting smaller and smaller.

The truth of this is borne out in statistics. In 1940, only 8 percent of the population lived alone, contrasted with 26 percent today.[1] Regarding the diminishing size of households generally, the United States Census Bureau reported:

> Households have decreased in size, with the most profound differences occurring at the extremes, the largest and smallest households...Between 1970 and 2000, households with five or more people decreased from 21 percent to 10 percent of all households. During the same period, the share of households with only one or two people increased from 46 percent to 59 percent. In addition, between 1970 and 2000 the average number of people per household declined from 3.14 percent to 2.62 percent.[2]

We talk about the assault on the family today. We recognize it by the divorce rate and the number of marriages that are in turmoil routinely. There's another aspect of assault that it seems we haven't considered. With the obvious rise in the single adult population, could it be that part of the devil's strategy to weaken and destroy the family unit is by negating it in the first place?

Shouldn't we be looking not only at the number of marriages dissolving, but also at the number *not forming* in contrast with past historical trends? I believe there is something to this, and it is one reason why I hope and pray that national family ministries as well as family ministries in local churches begin to take greater interest in the single population. We know part of the devil's strategy is to divide. Quite possibly, the decrease in family size, the increase in one-person households and the rising single population give us further evidence that he continues to push us away from one another. Is this one way we are seeing "people's love growing cold"? (See Matthew 24:12.)

INTENTIONAL COMMUNITY

So what are some ways you can improve your personal experience and build community within this current culture? The most obvious idea is you could once again, or perhaps for the first time, live with other singles. You can do this in all sorts of creative ways. Various factors such as age, budget and personality usually shape our choices. Some may choose to live in an apartment or condominium. Others may choose to share a house or split a duplex. Some may want only one roommate. Others may want a whole house full where there is a lot of activity and various friends coming and going.

Sure, having roommates can be challenging. For those who still have roommates—you may be experiencing these challenges now. Other people's habits can be irritating. Roommates can disappoint us by being irresponsible or hurt us by being insensitive. If you had some bad experiences, you might initially shudder at the thought of re-experiencing the roommate scene. But oftentimes, if we stop to really think about it, the benefits of living with others really can outweigh the challenges. If you exercise wisdom and discernment in your decisions concerning roommates and living arrangements, God can truly lead you into a sweet situation.

For those who are older, there are more ways to deal with common roommate challenges today than when you were in your twenties. For example, if you need your "space," keep in mind that combined incomes can often afford a bigger house, condominium or apartment. The increased use of cell phones and multiple telephone lines can probably solve most telephone issues. And remember that as we mature, most of us become more responsible and are in a better position to design workable plans regarding chores, food and shared expenses.

A significant advantage to having a roommate is that it's nice just having someone else around. It also allows you to share some meals with others. You can split housework with roommates, which frees up your time for other things. I also find that our motivation for maintaining a nicely decorated and well-kept home significantly increases when it is shared with others. Sharing it combats the "ho hum" attitude you easily fall prey to when you're the only one who regularly sees your home.

It is possible, and in various situations quite desirable, for single parents to have roommates. This can be tricky, because you not only have to blend adult personalities, but also those of your children. There are, however, numerous advantages to this type of shared living arrangement, one of which is a decreased financial commitment. If you have no children, living with a single parent can be a great source of joy and a great training ground for the future, should you have children later.

You also may consider living with a family. Here is the testimony of a missionary friend describing God's provision of her living arrangement with a family. "Homemade meals. Smiles of a one-year old. Encouragement of a friend and prayer partner. An old, country farmhouse warm with a family's love for each other and for the Lord. These are the blessings of my new home."[3]

Living with a family can be a great experience when expectations and boundaries are understood and respected. For example, a family needs to understand that you are not a nanny or a housekeeper, although you may choose to watch the children and do extra housework. On the other hand, you can't act like a guest—you must do your share as part of the household. When you work out the parameters, this can be a very desirable living arrangement.

For some who have left home, it actually might be good to move back in with your parents. While it is healthy and desirable for children to leave home and establish themselves apart from their parents, after this process occurs, it may be advantageous both to you and your parents to once again live together. If your relationship is good and healthy, this can be a real blessing to all.

Perhaps you prefer living alone. Or perhaps you'd love to have roommates, but cannot find a workable situation. You then may decide to reside near close friends, single or married.

This can be a great arrangement even if you do have room-mates! You can do this in a variety of ways. You can share a duplex or live in the same condominium or apartment complex. You can live on the same block or in the same neighborhood. The pivotal point is that you live in close proximity because it is easier to spend time with and feel the tangible support of friends living close by.

The advantages of this type of community living are numerous. You can share some meals with others easily. Spontaneous get-togethers are also easier. Brief visits that fit into small blocks of time are possible. When you need a helping hand, you feel more comfortable calling a friend who is just two blocks away than one who lives thirty minutes away. You can also derive comfort simply by knowing friends are near. "Better is a neighbor who is near than a brother far away" (Prov. 27:10).

Forming the type of living arrangement where a *group* of friends live relatively close is a safeguard against the formation of one-on-one codependent relationships. When you are knit within a group, there is less reason, less temptation to begin looking too much to one person to meet companionship needs. There is a healthy balance and healthy flow between multiple friends.

You must be *intentional* about working to develop a sense of community in your life. It's not going to just fall in your lap. You might have to move out of your current apartment, sell your house or take the risk of having roommates again. Making changes feels risky. But life simply is not risk free. To gain new ground, risk is almost always required. For every advance made in the last century, stop and consider that someone took a risk. When people are convinced that the goal is worth the risk, they push through the fears that otherwise hold them back.

Just imagine what it would be like if, when you came home, there was someone to greet you. Or if you as a single parent came home, and your roommate offered to care for your children while you went shopping or out with friends. How about finding out on Friday after work that a bunch of friends in the condominium complex were heading out to the movies? What if you regularly experienced the camaraderie and support we watch on *Friends*? You *can* improve your situation, but change requires work, and it does take risk. However, the rewards are worth it. Even the tough times are used for our good, to mold and shape us into the image of Christ. I challenge you to press through in this area. Be bold and daring in stepping out to develop a community life.

INVOLVEMENT IN HOME GROUPS OR OTHER SMALL GROUPS

In pursuing getting "connected" to a community, at the very least, you should be part of some sort of small group, whether that be a Bible study, a home group, some type of ministry group or other small group of Christian brothers and sisters. It's very difficult to develop meaningful relationships merely by attending a large service on Sunday morning. We all need to have a comfortable and safe context in which to meet and get to know people. Small groups provide that context.

Here are a few suggestions for developing meaningful relationships with small group members:

- Don't automatically write off the married people in the group as being folks with whom you cannot have a friendship. Be open. Get to know the people in the group as *people* first and foremost, not primarily as *married* or *single* people.

- Don't write off an entire group simply because it may be predominantly comprised of couples. Maybe you can be a groundbreaker, and more singles will follow behind you. Or maybe God has something special for you to give that group. Seek God's will about belonging to a group instead of allowing the marital status of the members to sway your decision.

- If you find yourself in a conversation predominantly geared around family issues, and you have no children, add insight with reflections from your own childhood experiences or from experiences you've shared with the children of friends or family. Don't succumb to feeling you are on the outside, having nothing to offer. Overcome that inclination by jumping into the conversation.

- During group discussions about the evening's teaching, interject examples or thoughts from your vantage point as a single. You can broaden the exposure of married members in helpful ways.

- If you are going out with some single friends after church, invite a married couple from your home group. Demonstrate and model bridging the gap.

- Organize a picnic or other group outing for all the group members. Often it just takes one person to get the ball rolling, and the next thing you know, you have an event where people are connecting and building friendships, both married and single.

- Take an active role in your group. Many groups share responsibilities among group members. Be a blessing by offering to serve in some capacity.

- Offer your home to host the group or periodically for some group activities, such as a game night or covered dish dinner.

- Offer to care for children and give a night out to some of the parents in your group.

These are just a few suggestions. There are many more things you can do to take the initiative to build community into your life. Be creative! Step out of the box! Don't do something just because that's the way it's always been done before.

Leaders of small groups need to be able to truly and effectively meet the needs of the singles in their care, and God can use *you* to help them know how. I've included a list below of some key ways in which leaders and group members can demonstrate genuine warmth and understanding to singles who visit or attend a small group. Ask the leader if you can discuss some of these suggestions with him or her. You may even decide to copy this list and give it to your leader. Present this information in a positive and encouraging manner, not in a way that implies fault on the part of your leader or other group members. We're all learning and growing, and God does not condemn us as we do.

- Be sensitive to the awkwardness singles may feel when entering a room full of couples or predominantly couples. Intentionally including us in conversation is one way to help ease this awkwardness. Draw us in.

- Recognize that it is uncomfortable for some singles to attend a group alone, especially for the first time. Greeting people near the entrance is a warm and welcoming thing for everyone and can make the initial solo entry of a single feel less stark.

- When using practical examples in a teaching, strive to incorporate examples pertinent to singles and not primarily just to couples and families.

- During fellowship time, if the discussion among couples tends to focus almost exclusively on some aspect of family life, try to steer the conversation so that it also includes aspects of life to which singles also relate. You can do this by peppering conversations with questions involving additional topics that you know might be of interest to the singles in attendance.

- Personally invite visiting singles to come back.

- Occasionally, make a point of praying as a group specifically for singles. Pray that God would bless us and satisfy our desires.

You can suggest that the leader encourage group members to do some of the following things outside of the group meeting to promote friendships with singles who attend your group:

- Invite a single to sit with you during a weekend service. This can be especially beneficial if you have a large sanctuary, because it can be difficult for singles to search out friends with whom to sit in a large auditorium. It is a horrible feeling to be at church, of all places, and feel alone in a crowd.

- Invite a single to go out with you after a weekend service or join you at home. A single's sense of aloneness is often heightened after leaving church as he or she watches many people leave in pairs or with their family.

- When some of the couples in the home group get together socially, invite some singles, too.

- Periodically offer to baby-sit for a single parent or offer other practical assistance.

- Invite a single over to dinner or on a family outing. Welcome those with whom you feel a genuine sense of rapport into your social circle.

Here's a success story related to home groups. A friend of mine found out that the leaders of her group, knowing that the singles in their group all wanted to be married, were regularly praying for this desire to be satisfied. When she and other singles in that group heard this, they were deeply touched. This displayed genuine caring on the part of these leaders toward the singles in their group.

As I make these suggestions, I am not at all implying that we are weak and need couples to take us by the hand and help us

along, as if we cannot do it for ourselves. This is demeaning.
The suggestions above are meant to *enhance* our experience in a
home group, to make it *easier* and more comfortable for us to
attend, and to give practical examples of simple ways we can
bridge the gap between couples and singles.

BE PERSONALLY INVOLVED IN YOUR CHURCH

Last but not least, I want to encourage you to get plugged in
to your church. The church is a family. Within families,
people both give and receive. It becomes problematic if a person is usually serving and never being served, or usually
receiving but rarely giving. All things in balance!

I know of singles who have worked very hard to get connected in their churches. Despite the cultural hindrances,
they've rolled up their sleeves and plowed on through anyway. Those singles are to be commended. Be encouraged,
and keep at it. You are a role model to others—both to singles and couples.

> Let your light shine before men in such a way that
> they may see your good works, and glorify your
> Father who is in heaven.
>
> —MATTHEW 5:16

Some people may misjudge singles, but by your actions you
can gently show them a different side of singleness—perhaps
one they've never seen.

I know there are also those who feel they've given and given
and received little back. That's rough. If you get to the point
of resentment, you need to resolve some boundary issues.
Only you, by seeking God, can determine where the line
should be drawn.

On the other hand, I know of singles who don't take initiative
to get involved. *Like all people groups*, singles are comprised of
those who do their share of giving and those who don't. It is my

prayer that those who tend to sit more on the sidelines will become motivated to pitch in and do their part. Don't be like the slave who hid his talent in the ground instead of multiplying it. (See Matthew 25:14–30.) The parable implies that the slave made this poor decision because he had a distorted view of his master and was fearful (Matt. 25:25).

Fear is one of the obstacles that keeps some singles on the sidelines—fear of rejection, failure, the lack of provision and resources or of intimacy. Jesus understands our fears, but He doesn't allow us to use them to justify our lack of involvement. Instead He promises to help us conquer them. From Genesis to Revelation, He repeatedly says, "Fear not." (There are sixty-two biblical instances of that exact phrase, and over three hundred verses that address the subject of fear.) In Isaiah 41:13, He specifically says, "Do not fear, *I will help you*" (emphasis added). Trust God to help you. Ask Him to send you the resources you need to overcome whatever holds you back from involvement. As He answers your prayers and sends resources your way, give yourself fully to His transforming process. As your fears abate, begin getting involved. Pick up the phone; make the call. Fill out the volunteer form. Sign the pledge. Make a commitment; then keep your word.

Every person has something valuable to give. As you pitch in, relationships will form. That might not happen immediately, but stay faithful. In this arena as in all others, take initiative. Don't yield to the faulty mentality that the married people are "in charge" and singles sit off to the side. Various things in our culture can make us feel this way. This isn't a blatant thought—it is so subtle you might not even realize it is influencing you. Take a mental inventory and assess whether you may have come under this without even knowing it. If you have, throw it off, and then get going!

No matter how you go about building community into your life, you have to go into it with your eyes open. Relationships are hard. We all sin. Plus, we're all different.

There will be challenges. But you are in a better position to deal with them if you go into this effort knowing challenges are *sure* to come. Then when they do, you won't be surprised. Instead you'll realize that encountering relational trials is normal. Working through differences with others is simply part of growing and maturing.

Challenging times with roommates and friends are the grounds whereon Jesus often calls us to die to our "flesh" so that His life can flow through us. (See John 12:24; Romans 8:13; Galatians 5:16–26.) It is not fun dying to our selfishness (Heb. 12:11). Yet, we must. This is all part of being conformed into the wonderful image of Christ (Rom. 8:29). So stay committed when the going gets rough. Let Jesus be Lord, and let Him call the shots (Luke 6:46; Matt. 7:21).

Chapter 17

Tipped Scales

Do you think the church seems like a "couples' church"? If you do, you are not alone. Did you know that the editors of *Christianity Today* thought this was enough of a problem to devote the entire June 2001 issue to this subject? What was the title of that issue? "Living Single in a Couples Church."[1] And this quote from a single is prominently displayed on a website for a church in Milwaukee, Wisconsin: "I don't fit in at church. It seems that everyone else is part of a family."[2]

In her book *Single and Content*, Lana Trent writes, "The church doesn't realize how many people avoid services because they are too focused on families and alienate singles."[3] Here's a revealing book title: *Single Adults Want to Be the Church, Too* by Britton Wood. In an article entitled "Why Singles Boycott Churches" published in *BreakPoint* on January 7, 2002, Julia Duin writes:

> Even at the more sophisticated megachurches, pastors assume that all those listening to their sermons who are over thirty are married. If they mention singles at all, it's with the adjective "young" in front of them.[4]

Speaking of church announcements, Duin writes, "Most... come with the assumption you are there as a family unit."[5]

Renewal Radio ministry published an article entitled "Singled Out in Church" in the February 2002 issue of *Encourager*. The author, Mark Chalemin, wrote:

> Hollywood almost ignores the reality that half of the adults in the United States are married. They seem to glorify...the single lifestyle and, in the process, minimize the existence and value of the married population. Now, let's take a look at the traditional church in

191

the United States. We often see a picture *equally* out of balance in the *opposite* direction. Churches tend to offer programs and sermons that often minimize or virtually ignore the half of all adults in our country who are single.[6]

Perhaps you have become increasingly more aware of feeling overlooked or on the sidelines of the church. This sense seems to be growing as the 2000 census statistics are becoming more widely known. In an article entitled "When Recruiting, Don't Forget Singles," Richard Gentzler, director of adult ministries for the United Methodist General Board of Discipleship, said, "If ministry is directed only to married people, we are ignoring nearly one-half of our adult population. As the church seeks to meet the challenges of a new century, we must widen our perspective of ministry and gain insight and understanding into the needs and concerns of single adults."[7]

It is important to gain this insight, because not only do some singles feel overlooked, but worse still, some feel used. They feel as if the church has been happy to have their help, yet has continuously ignored or downplayed their needs. Another quote from the aforementioned church website reads: "Because I'm single, my church seems to expect that I should be able to give more money and more time than people who are married. They don't realize that when you're alone you don't have anyone to share in the expenses or the chores."[8]

Some have grown bitter and turned away. Speaking of singles leaving the church, Julia Duin said:

> I've seen the same pattern all over the country: committed evangelical Christian men and women in their thirties and forties who have had it with their family-centric churches and who have quietly slipped out.
>
> More and more Christian singles are quietly boycotting their churches…They have put in twenty or more years of service to their churches and have gotten

> little or nothing back….these are real singles who have
> put up and put out and have now opted out of an irrel-
> evant church…[They] are smart, together people and
> their boycott…is a huge loss to the body of Christ.[9]

Sadly, the whole church is being impacted negatively by this problem.

It is very likely that your church looks very different through a married person's eyes than through yours. This is because we each experience church from our cultural perspective. The lives of married persons align with that of most of our church leaders and the norm generally depicted in the church. So it's easy for them to miss the fact that some things often portrayed in the church as normative are not normative to you. One of the pastors of my church, Dr. Steve Robbins, explains that the reason people often can't see a problem in their culture is because "we perceive *through* our culture rather than stand over against it; therefore, analysis is difficult at best." In other words, unless you step *outside* of your culture, your view of it is biased by living *in* it. So to a great degree, this problem of imbalance is undetected and therefore quite unintentional.

OUT-OF-BALANCE FOCUS

Despite being unintentional, this out-of-balance focus of attention is causing growing division between singles and couples in the church. To correct the lack of balance, you first have to see it more clearly. When you do, God can use you to help others see it so we can bring about needed changes. It is observable in three primary areas:

- Leadership
- Resources and materials
- Attention given

Leadership imbalance

Outside of leaders in the Catholic church, can you think of any single who is currently leading a national or international

ministry? Can you think of any nationally known congregation whose pastor is single? Let's take this a step closer to
home. Can you think of any single who is currently leading a
successful ministry in your community or who is a pastor of a
local church in your area? Do you know of any single who is
serving as a deacon or as a member of a board of trustees,
church council or presbytery? How about one who is serving
in some other significant position of leadership in your
church, or a church or ministry in your community? If you
can, great! Certainly some single leaders can be found.

But now take a moment to contrast this with the number of
married persons filling those same types of roles. Striking difference, isn't there? George Barna reports that 94 percent of
our Protestant pastors are married, and it would not surprise
me if the ratio of married to single people filling other types
of high levels of leadership in the church is similar.

Think about this: Almost half your community is single.
Yet so few leaders in the Protestant church are single. Paul
was a magnificent role model, demonstrating that God has
not excluded singles from high levels of leadership in the
church. Likewise, the entire Catholic tradition stands on the
credo of single leadership. So what's causing this imbalance?

You may raise the issue of age, thinking that too many singles are either too young or too old to fill these leadership
roles. But age is not a viable cause of the low ratio of single to
married leaders. Only 25 percent of singles are between the
ages of twenty to twenty-nine. Only 15 percent are age sixty-
five and above.[10] Besides, many strong leaders start young and
finish old.

Even as a single, you may think that there simply are not
enough *mature* singles to be placed in these types of higher
leadership positions. Your view may be biased by the unfortunate stereotype. Almost half the population can't realistically
be less mature than the other half simply because of marital
status. God is conforming *you* into His image as He also is

conforming married people. He uses the vehicles of singleness and marriage as crucibles to perform that transforming process.

All of these points tell us something is wrong. When the sheer numbers from which to draw leaders is almost the same for singles as for the married population, and when there is not a theological prohibition against singles in leadership, the reality in the church today stands out clearly as a concern.

In "Singled Out in Church," Mark Chalemin, wrote: "It is remarkable that the world places single adults in charge of departments and entire corporations, but many times the church does not consider these very same people for leadership positions."[11]

This imbalance is one reason the church seems like a "couples' church." We think of leaders as a reflection of the people choosing to follow them. Additionally, leaders echo back their experience, so that married perspective also makes the church seem like a couples' church.

Singles issues resources

Another area of imbalance is the availability of resources and materials addressing issues commonly faced by couples vs. singles. We have just as great a need for guidance and sound teaching about how to "do life" while single as couples do about learning to "do life" married. Yet there are a lot less resources for us than there are for couples.

To compare the availability of books, I performed a search on the website of two leading booksellers. On Christianbook.com, a search using their subcategory "Singles and Dating," which is found under the main category "Marriage and Parenting," yielded forty-two books. A search using the keyword "Singles" yielded fifty-nine books. The "Marriage" category yielded 619 books.

On Amazon.com, under "Religion and Spirituality/ Christianity/Christian Living/Relationships," their established category for "Dating and the Single Life" yielded 149 books and "Marriage" yielded 1,222 books.[12] Gauging by these searches, 10 percent or less of the books on these two subjects are directed to singles. Thank God for the countless ways in which the materials provided for couples have aided them and likely saved many marriages. But we see from the ratio that there truly is a hole to fill for singles.

Here's the complicating factor, though, which we cannot lose sight of because it comes up again and again. Many of us don't want to read a "singles book" because we don't want to be single! This explains, in part, the inequity between books on the topic of marriage vs. being single. This complication, however, does not negate the need to provide teaching to singles about "doing life" for the period that we are single. This situation is analogous to trying to talk someone into eating a bowl of spinach when he or she hates spinach! We'll look at ways to resolve this problem later.

Next, let's think about some of the national ministries that are devoted to strengthening marriage and family life. Some of the big and generally well-known ministries are Focus on the Family, Family Life Today, the Family Research Council, American Family Association and PromiseKeepers.[13] Focus on the Family has a staff of thirteen hundred, an annual budget of $128 million and a circulation of 2.6 million for their monthly magazine, *Focus on the Family*.[14] The Family Research Council has a staff of one hundred, an annual budget of $11.5 million and a circulation of one hundred ten thousand for their monthly publication, *Washington Watch*.[15] According to the Family Life Today website, since its founding in 1976, over one million people have attended their conferences, and they have a lay volunteer network of over ten thousand couples.[16]

In contrast, national singles ministries are not as well known, promoted or followed as these family ministries. There is the Network of Single Adult Leaders, the United Methodist Single Adult Leaders, Single Life Resources and the North American Conference of Separated and Divorced

Catholics, Inc. In many respects, these organizations just have a smaller "feel" to them than those listed above for family ministries. For example, the Network of Single Adult Leaders has a staff of one, an annual budget of $75,000 and a membership of one thousand.[17] The North American Conference of Separated and Divorced Catholics, Inc. has a staff of one, an annual budget of $124,000, a membership of two thousand and a circulation of four thousand for its quarterly magazine, *Jacob's Well*.[18] Those who don't find singles ministries in their local churches appealing also generally don't care to follow national singles organizations either.

The difference in the availability of conferences and magazines for couples vs. singles is also stark.[19] And when you see a reference to or offering for marriage or family on websites, bookstores, church lobbies or church bulletins, often there is no corresponding reference or offering for singles. Or if there is, it is not obvious. Once you have eyes to see, you realize how off balance the church really is.

Another area of imbalance in attention occurs in churches that make a practice of inviting people to receive prayer for various needs after a sermon or at some other time during a service or conference. The announced topics of prayer sometimes involve issues that arise in marriage and parenting but, in contrast, rarely touch upon issues common to us. For example, an invitation to receive prayer may be announced for couples struggling in their marriages, on the brink of divorce or who have not been able to conceive. Sadly, we seldom hear an invitation to receive prayer for those who are grieving a broken relationship or engagement, mourning as they pass the childbearing years or struggling with loneliness or rejection. I believe *God's heart breaks* when we are inadvertently overlooked. When you feel overlooked, remember that Jesus sees your need; it is not *unnoticed*.

Church teaching

My last point is on the subject of inclusion of references and examples pertinent to singles in all kinds of teaching offered by pastors and other church leaders. It is critical that I describe the attitude with which I approach this subject. I hold a deep and abiding respect for the pastors and other church leaders in our country. I believe that God is the one who establishes authority. "For there is no authority except from God, and those which exist are established by God" (Rom. 13:1; cf. Dan. 2:21; 4:17; John 19:11; 1 Pet. 2:13–14). When God truly is the One who has called, anointed and equipped a leader, that should elicit our respect. (See also Hebrews 13:17; 1 Timothy 5:17; cf. Philippians 2:29; 1 Corinthians 16:16–18.) I believe that the majority of leaders who truly are called by God do serve God and us earnestly and with integrity. It is with this attitude that I bring the next subject to the forefront. I'm going to point out some areas of weakness, but not from a malicious, critical or "fault-finding" heart. My goal and purpose in addressing the next subject is to support and give practical assistance to pastors and other leaders.

Unfortunately, sermons and teachings are principal contributors to the sense of imbalance we feel. Although much is said that applies to people across the board regardless of our differences, there's a noticeable disparity between the frequency of references or experiences specifically applicable to couples vs. singles.

We also feel the imbalance when pastors teach a series on marriage or parenting sometimes lasting between three to six weekend sermons, possibly every year or two. But we don't hear a series on being single, perhaps not even one entire message. While the church *needs* teachings on marriage and parenting, we also need *balance*. We need more teachings that specifically address our challenges.

This issue of needed balance in teachings is generally true at all levels—at the small group level all the way up to the national level. It is true in local and national radio broadcasts given by Christian teachers. It is true in local and national men's and women's conferences.

This imbalance is understandable because leaders naturally draw upon their own life experiences when using practical examples to make a point. Additionally, most married pastors lack the personal experience necessary to *intrinsically* understand our challenges. For example, only 12 percent have experienced divorce.[20] We cannot expect them to just "know" what it's like to be single. Speaking about married pastors, Mark Chalemin said, "This lack of personal experience and relational distance regarding singles results in an unintentional lack of awareness and persistent gap in understanding of singles and their lifestyle."[21]

There are additional, reasonable explanations for the focus on families we see in today's church. The most important is because there *needs* to be a focus on families! Much in the secular culture communicates a questionable and sometimes negative message about marriage. We are aware of the increasing divorce rate. Working to turn the tide and hold families together has noticeably placed much focus on families, which should be sustained. However, shoring up families need not and should not be done at our expense, but actually with our support and strengthening abilities. As family, we are here to encourage and support one another—to pull together as a *team* for God's purposes, which in turn pleases and glorifies Him.

The imbalance also has been caused by the fact that the church hasn't noticed a gradual shift in the population, so we've continued our same methods of relating and communicating. What was appropriate forty years ago, however—when almost 70 percent of the population were married—no longer works in today's world. Now that we are aware of today's demographics and changing needs, we must respond. Just as the church responded upon recognizing the new threats and challenges being imposed on married couples, the church must likewise respond to the difficulties imposed on us—many of which, unfortunately, actually emanate from the church itself.

A repeating cycle of how we choose and prepare upcoming leaders has also contributed to our current imbalance. Due to today's gap between couples and singles, married leaders tend to gravitate toward other married persons to mentor as upcoming leaders. This naturally results from their more frequent social interactions. Opportunities to spot leadership traits in singles are not as common. Thus, the cycle for grooming upcoming leaders remains predominantly in the couples' domain. Concerted effort must be made to break out of this cycle.

Despite the understandable reasons for this imbalance, it sends a negative message to us, which is something I'm certain both God and our church leaders want to correct.

Chapter 18

Judge a Tree by Its Fruit

You may be very conscious of the imbalance in the church, or fairly unconscious, or somewhere in between. Wherever you fall on that spectrum, your level of awareness shapes your views of yourself and the church.

If you're very conscious of the imbalance, you may interpret actions (or inaction) of the church as indicators that your pastors or other church leaders don't care about you specifically or singles generally or, at best, are aloof to you or to singles. I understand your vantage point. If week after week your pastor routinely makes references to things pertaining to marriage and parenting and hardly ever references singles, what are you to think?

This lack of communication is a wide-open door to fill the "blank spaces" with wrong assumptions. Over time, you may begin to believe what is *perceived* more than reality. Unfortunately, you can even start perceiving things to be worse than they actually are by filtering everything through glasses that negatively color your view. Obviously, if this festers, it can drive a wedge between you and your leaders. Left unchecked, this negativity can spread like gangrene (1 Cor. 5:6).

It is difficult to turn around a *perceived* lack of caring. "A brother offended is harder to be won than a strong city, and contentions are like the bars of a castle" (Prov. 18:19). If this perception continues, the circumstances are ripe for strife. "For the churning of milk produces butter, and pressing the nose brings forth blood; so the churning of anger produces strife" (Prov. 30:33).

I believe that almost every leader would like to turn this perception around. If your pastor became aware of this problem *and knew how to resolve it*, he or she would do it! We all know it is tragic when a son or daughter wrongly believes his or her parents don't love him or her merely because of a breakdown in communication. We yearn to remedy this type of situation when hearing of it because it's so needless—the hurt is founded on untruth. As the church remedies this area of shortfall, you will become more alive and vibrant with renewed hope and a greater sense of significance. Since we all, as family, have an affect on one another, ultimately this helps the whole church!

Despite the clear imbalance, you, like couples, might not actually have seen it before I described it because you're so accustomed to it. Living *in* the culture makes it difficult to look *at* it. Even if you haven't seen it, you've *felt* it. It's caused a reaction inside, but you don't link the reaction to the imbalance because you weren't aware of it. The felt perception of the imbalance may have produced several things in you. First, the focus on marriage may have *heightened your desire to marry*. In part this is because, by depicting marriage as the norm, the church indirectly "tells" you that you *should* be married. Also, because you want to feel and be regarded as normal, another thing this imbalance may have produced in you is routine questioning as to whether something is wrong with you since you don't fit the depicted norm. Perhaps you feel odd or out of place. All the more, then, this imbalance may drive you toward marriage so that you'll feel normal and fit in.

Although unintentional, the imbalanced focus on family sends a message without words that, other than being devoted to God, getting married and raising a family are the principal aims of life. This can leave you feeling left out of the mainstream. Sure, you tell yourself that this is not the aim of life, for your Christian theology informs you otherwise. Yet the primary model of life the church holds before you does not seem to back that up. So you may feel caught between two realities—that of theology and that of true-life experience. Left unchecked, this is another area where you may be tempted to believe the perception more than reality. You can cave in to feeling you are on the sidelines and married folks are the main players.

What the imbalance conveys to you is especially important with respect to the issue of Christian leadership. Because most of the church's leaders are married, this seems to say, again without words, that you must be married to lead—that being single disqualifies you from leadership. If you are a single woman in a church in which the primary avenue of leadership for women is alongside their husbands, you may feel this even more poignantly.

The emphasis you see on marriage and parenting, coupled with the lack of single leaders who demonstrate a different lifestyle that also glorifies God and serves His people, may hit you like a double whammy. For the sake of healing and bringing about change in the church, it is important that you clearly see these two major ways that the church has failed singles:

- It (inadvertently) focuses our attention on marriage.

- It doesn't tangibly show us another way.

It is even more important that in seeing this, you not grow bitter or become a faultfinder. We can't throw stones. The church is imperfect because it's made up of imperfect people. That's why we *all* need God! Yet, God doesn't call us to ignore what's wrong either. *Only by seeing this reality do we better understand why some singles place much emphasis on wanting to get married and seemingly not enough on making the most of being single.* You may have been faulted for this by some leaders—leaders who didn't recognize that the church has played a part in producing this. Forgive them, and as God opens doors, help them see what they didn't understand.

The imbalance also plays a role in producing several quandaries for singles in the area of contentment. On one hand, the church *continually stirs* our desire for marriage through the ongoing focus on families. On the other hand, it admonishes us to "be content." Through an indirect message the church *fuels the fire, and then pours water on it* by the direct message to "be content." This can be a bit maddening. Church leaders likely have some role in you moving back and forth on the contentment continuum.

The imbalance and all the confusing messages it inadvertently conveys cumulatively have an insidious way of implying *negative* things about being single. *So is it any wonder that you may struggle with being discontent?* No one wants to live under that cloud. It is indeed a high challenge to be content with a lifestyle the church itself, albeit inadvertently, seems to ignore or even to portray as abnormal.

In reaction to all these things, if you have consciously felt marginalized, you may then push to gain "equal" recognition or prominence with that of families, almost as if you're in competition. While it is good to seek balance, it must be done in love, not in a competitive spirit. "Let all that you do be done in love" (1 Cor. 16:14). Anything done with an underlying spirit of competition is sure to cause problems for all—singles and couples alike.

If you've not consciously felt marginalized but do feel out of place, you may strive to find or create a place of belonging, not finding it in the church generally. This is what sometimes spurs the creation of a singles ministry. While it is critical that you feel a sense of belonging in the church, you must be careful in your approach. *All* singles need to feel that the *entire* church is a "place" where they belong.

Constant focus on families with little focus on singles creates a real temptation to develop a "have or have not" mentality. You may view yourself as a "have not," as if to say to families, "You have it all: the spouse, the children, the home, and you are the hub of the church." You may view couples as being unaware of, aloof to and unaffected by the challenges and hardships singles face. You may subtly feel this, or it may be full blown. If you allow these kinds of thoughts to fester, a storm brews. But Jesus wants to calm the storm! Let Him minister to you and heal the wounds that have led to this.

In reaction to the exclusion some singles feel, I've heard the suggestion that we develop a singles church. I was saddened by this. Such division is not God's way. Yet His heart does ache over the things singles have experienced that caused this idea to be conceived.

Certainly God wants to correct and make right the things about the church today that have provoked people to the point of suggesting a separate church. However, God also calls us beyond division and the things that provoke us. He graces us to respond in ways that are pleasing to Him. We must emphatically reject the "us vs. them" mentality. It does not matter how much you may feel you've been overlooked or belittled. God calls us to unity! A house divided against itself cannot stand (Matt. 12:25). Others in history have felt left out of the mainstream. For example, many African Americans, when treated as inferior, exhibited incredible, commendable character in the face of insult, even after a long history of atrocities endured by their race.

Costa Mitchell, a leading pastor and church planter of Vineyard churches in South Africa, tells a true story about Nelson Mandela that holds a great analogy for us. In South Africa, rugby had always been the "white man's sport." In the apartheid years, the Anti-Apartheid movements sanctioned the national teams, and blacks were unable to take part in World Cup events. One year at a World Cup rugby final, Nelson Mandela went out onto the field wearing the jersey of Francois Pienaar, the South Africa captain, uniting South Africa behind him and the team. He began leading other blacks in cheering and supporting the team and the sport, which for years had excluded them. That event, to many South Africans, stands out as a day of reconciliation, breaking down walls between blacks and whites. What an incredible display of character and leadership.

You may feel disenfranchised. I understand that. But we must rise above in the same way Mandela modeled it for us. Mandela was modeling what Jesus modeled for us. A beautiful, God-etched character can throw down feelings of being left holding the bag, *even* when people don't understand or seem to care how you feel. Choose to rally behind the families in your church whether they understand your pain or not. When you accepted Jesus Christ's righteousness, you did not understand the pain He went through to give it to you. But He did it anyway. Our actions should be righteous whether or not people understand what it takes to respond that way.

I attended a concert by Twila Paris, where she shared that she and her husband had not been able to conceive a child, to their deep disappointment. Yet God moved her to produce a compact disc of lullabies. I listened with tears as she said she felt it was one of the most moving works she has produced. Despite her lack, her unfulfilled desire, she chose to be a blessing to everyone else's children. Now that is something God will indeed anoint. It takes amazing grace to decide to turn and be a blessing to the very ones you are tempted to envy or even despise. God loves to give this kind of amazing grace to those who are willing to walk in it. Not only that, but sometimes He also afterward gives us the desire of our hearts. Twila Paris did, in fact, give birth to a child some time later.

You may not be at a place where you can give this kind of response. The wound is too deep; the hurt is too fresh; the sore is too raw. I understand. God wants to heal those wounds and bring you, even to your surprise, to the place where, amazingly, you actually will be able to respond in a similar manner as depicted in these two examples. Meanwhile, those of us who are strong enough to bear the burdens of the weak should lead the charge and pave the way for others who just can't quite find the inner strength or resolve to get behind this yet.

In this spirit of resolve and unity, we turn to the next subject—how to bring balance to the church.

Chapter 19

Adding More Weight to the Other Side

Will you be a change agent in your church? This chapter suggests practical things your church can do to make singles feel just as much a part of the body as couples and explains why these changes are advocated. Use this chapter as a manual. Arrange meetings with your pastors and other church leaders to discuss the recommendations here. Respectfully explain your perspective, and listen to theirs as well. Offer your assistance in implementing the changes you advocate. Present yourself as a team player. You are there to unify, so you must be conciliatory and understanding.

You may want to discuss the concepts of this chapter with other singles in your church before speaking to church leaders. Gain insight from them, and represent their views when you talk with leaders. First, get a firm grasp of the content of this chapter; then help others understand it.

Ask God to open doors to the right people—those He will use to usher in these positive changes. Ask Him to give you favor in their eyes and to help you clearly articulate these concepts. Pray for wisdom and guidance every step of the way.

THE POWER OF THE PULPIT

The most significant and powerful way to shift the balance and give greater attention to singles is for pastors to incorporate into their sermons more references and examples that relate directly to singles. Pastors are in the best position to influence the largest number of people in their congregations. This approach also has the most immediate effect.

First, let's look at the direct impact on singles. When you believe your own pastor understands and values you and is sensitive to your struggles, the effect is profound. Pastors generally hold a great degree of importance in our lives. Consequently it can be very touching and powerful when they convey that they understand you.

I remember when my pastor related a story about how a single person felt when introduced to a friend's friend. He mentioned what the single person was thinking—*Oh, no, did you have to mention that I was single? Now he's probably wondering what's wrong with me...*

When I heard my pastor tell this story, I thought, *Oh, he understands! He really understands!* There was an instant connection and instant comfort I felt from him at a level I had not felt prior to that point. He validated me—my feelings and experiences. He showed his compassion. This meant so much to me. I know this same type of experience can be duplicated over and over in our churches. And when it is, you and other singles will thrive like never before!

To extend this even further, I believe great results would flow from a pastor's decision to teach a series specifically on the subject of being single. There are so many facets to being single. Because singles are so diverse, teaching on the subject requires sufficient time to address the issues applicable to our diverse situations and various life stages. An in-depth understanding is needed, especially now when we have had so little exposure to these types of subjects.

Let's look at this from another angle. Pastors address difficult issues about living as a married person to which you relate from a different vantage point. Your pastor can powerfully impact the singles in your church by tying these together. For example, I've heard pastors discuss how hard it is when a couple wanting children is unable to conceive. I can really relate to this because I know the pain of desperately wanting to have children yet being in a position where I cannot. I know the agony of continuously hoping, hoping, hoping, and then gradually watching the opportunity slip away with age. So, rather than merely talking about the difficulties experienced by a couple, your pastor also can mention the hardship we may face with respect to this issue. Greater pain results when the subject of a couple's difficulty is brought up. Yet our pain, our longings are never mentioned. You may feel totally overlooked, and your pastor certainly does not intend this.

A single man approached me after I began teaching seminars on singles issues. He said he felt that pastors don't understand what it feels like to be single. Among other things, he gave me the following example. He said that in a particular sermon, a pastor expressed how much he missed his wife while away on a trip. He was lonely without her. The single man told me that he has lived with this type of longing day in and day out for years.

The single man felt incensed. The pastor described difficulties couples in a good marriage face when separated, yet made no mention of what singles endure as they face, not a short period of longing like this, but years of it. You can imagine how powerful it could have been for the singles in this pastor's congregation had he simply inserted, even parenthetically, a comment expressing that he understands how singles must feel routinely. This would have been a simple modification to his sermon, yet its impact could have been so significant. But that opportunity was missed likely because the pastor just didn't see the need or possible analogy.

Even in their specific teachings on marriage or parenting, pastors have three distinct golden opportunities to apply the teaching to us. First, they can sincerely state that the message is pertinent to us for the day we too may marry. If this is said with enthusiasm and hope-filled words, it means a lot to you, doesn't it? It can lift your spirits, which is especially helpful if the sermon is tough for you to hear.

Pastors can increase their impact if they also include a

sensitive statement expressing an understanding of how some singles in their congregation might feel about listening to this type of sermon. Unfortunately, much of the time, nothing like that is added, or worse, a pastor makes light of the feelings of singles. Jokes of this nature trivialize the seriousness and pain of the subject, and this can *wound* us.

Third, a pastor can explain and give practical examples of how we can be a wonderful part of the picture in the life of a family! By so doing, everybody learns about family-based friendships. And when a pastor points out the value of your involvement in a family, the teaching suddenly comes alive right there and then—where you are *that* day—not just down the road if you marry. Suddenly, a teaching that may have seemed almost irrelevant to you or painful takes on new meaning. And by this, pastors no longer leave out half the congregation when speaking on the subject of marriage or parenting. Everybody wins!

When we are incorporated in more balanced ways into things pastors say from the pulpit, it conveys our importance and significance. It also communicates that being single is normal instead of an anomaly. A simple change like this will breathe new life and hope into you and other singles in your congregation, which in turn will produce greater health and stability. The stronger we are, the better equipped we are to fulfill the roles to which God has called us. The natural by-product is a healthier and stronger church.

Here's another very significant reason we need to hear about singles issues directly from the pulpit. As I explained earlier, many of us don't want to read singles books, go to singles meetings or participate in national singles ministries because we don't want to be single. Nevertheless, we *need* teaching to address our specific areas of struggle. If you avoid opportunities to be taught because you can't stand the subject or the context for the teaching, how else will you hear things that genuinely help unless you hear it from the pulpit? If necessary aids, good examples and helpful analogies relevant to singles were peppered into sermons regularly, you would be better taught than you are now concerning singles issues.

Another reason we need pastors to speak about singles issues from the pulpit is to help couples see why it is important that they understand our issues. If couples understand the importance, they will more likely be motivated to devote time and energy to become better educated about these issues. A pastor's input lends credibility and purpose to this overall message.

NECESSARY PREPARATION

We now come to an unpleasant, but important reason why we need more training in the church regarding living as a single, which I explain by contrast. It is helpful for you to learn in advance about marriage to be better prepared should you marry. The opposite is also true. Couples benefit from learning more about being single to be better prepared if and when they someday find themselves single. Quite understandably, no one likes to think about this. We don't like to contemplate bad things that might happen. That's why we procrastinate doing things like having a will drawn up, making a financial plan for our senior years or purchasing disability insurance. But it is prudent to have a plan for days of adversity, and we are wise to acknowledge that with age comes the inevitable.

As a church, we do a *service* to people by helping them know better how to cope with adversity when it comes. Losing a spouse is hard enough without adding the sudden jolt of facing an entirely different way of life for which you are not prepared. We can help those who find themselves single again if they are at least exposed to teaching on the subject before they ever arrive at that unfortunate juncture.

Shifting to the other side of the chronological continuum, pastors need to speak a word to parents. Most parents envision their children being happily married and having wonderful children. This is the *ideal* many parents desire for their children. They talk as if all their children will get married. No one ever says to his or her child, "Someday, when you are living alone…" No! Parents routinely say, "Someday, when you're married and have your own children…"

But statistics indicate marriage may not come until much later in life. We do our children a disservice if we don't prepare them for this real possibility. Part of the reason I have struggled so much as a single is because no one prepared me to live the single life. Everyone assumed I'd get married. Parents don't like to think of the possibility of extended singleness for their children, but they need to. Parents prepare their children for other types of difficulties so they'll know what to do in challenging situations. They don't like to think of their teenagers behind the wheel in a bad snowstorm, yet they teach them how to drive through one. In principle, it is no different with respect to being single. Many aspects of being single are not pleasant. You may find yourself thinking, *Yeah, but how in the world do you prepare someone to be single?* By thinking that, you prove the necessity of a book like this and the fact that we need more teaching that reaches everyone—singles, couples, young, old—*everyone.*

TRAINING FOR CHURCH LEADERS

While hearing from the pulpit is an important and necessary first step in bringing balance to the church, much more can be done. Another necessity is to train other married church leaders about singles issues. Those who teach can then begin incorporating more references to singles issues into their teachings. Those who lead in other capacities can begin looking for ways to incorporate more singles into their various spheres of influence.

Church leaders are usually the next tier down from pastors in terms of having influence in the congregation. The more they understand the relevance and value of integrating us into the congregation, and the more they understand about us, the more God can use them to model new ways of relating and communicating with us. First and foremost, leaders need to begin developing a new mind-set about us and about the church's approach to us. As they do so, they'll naturally incorporate changes in their own lives and then pass that enthusiasm on to others.

Church leaders typically are very busy people, so efficient ways to provide this type of training must be utilized. Most churches have periodic leaders' meetings or retreats. Training about singles issues could be given at these meetings. More information could be disseminated in written form, through newsletters, letters from the pastor or through articles that can be distributed easily via e-mail. Seminars addressing specific singles issues could be provided on tape or compact disc so leaders can multitask—drive and listen, prepare dinner and listen, and so on. Where there is a will, there is a way!

Change also will be encouraged through another group of people—those in whom God already has placed a burden regarding these issues. Their motivation is internal, emanating from the Holy Spirit. Some of these folks will be leaders and others will not. Either way, God will powerfully use them! Pastors and other church leaders would do well to actively try to identify who these people are and then "deputize" them to be change-agents in the church. They should be supported, encouraged and given the tools they need.

GET THE MESSAGE OUT

Finally, leaders need to just put the teaching out there, taking the approach, "Whosoever, come!" Slowly but surely, with God behind this effort, people will begin taking greater interest, and concepts will spread. Seminars on topics pertinent to singles can be offered. These can be recorded and offered over the Internet. If your church offers marriage seminars or other types of marriage training classes, the leader can periodically include

teachings about forming and maintaining friendships with singles and other relevant and related topics to help bridge the gap
between couples and singles.

From time to time, your church can include articles in peri-
odicals it publishes. This book could be used for discussions in
Bible studies and other types of small groups. Special teachings
regarding singles can be given at various church conferences,
such as women's and men's conferences and conferences
devoted to other topics that lend themselves to teachings of
this nature. When such teaching is offered, encourage leaders
to use descriptions referring to issues affecting people *during
the time they are single*. This helps to take the label off. It helps
to eliminate the view that "single" is who you *are* and the
mind-set that your singleness is permanent.

If your church announces topics for which people may wish
to receive prayer after a service, remind leaders to remember
the challenges facing singles. Our needs must be given similar
attention. Singles will feel great compassion through this
recognition, which will produce healing. I personally believe
this matter is of *great importance* to God. I have sometimes felt
a sense of His longings for singles during prayer times,
accompanied by an emptiness and *deep* sadness when our
issues have not been recognized. I believe that some very special evidence of God's answers to our prayers will come forth
when recognition of these needs is expressed and invitations
for prayer for singles issues become much more common.

Another means by which the church can become more balanced is in general communication with people. Examine the
various media through which your church communicates with
its members and the public. Consider ways in which your
church can express information pertaining to singles in ways
similar to that for families. For example, if your church has a
website, look it over. Does it have a special link or tab for marriage and family issues? Is there a corresponding identifier for
singles? If not, suggest that one be added. Personally, I

recommend it be incorporated right in with marriage and family life to more poignantly convey our integration. Make sure the information given communicates the church's view of singles and clearly communicates the church's desire to incorporate us in all manners in the church, not merely through the avenue of "singles ministry" as we have always known it. Walk through your church's lobby. What is it saying to couples—to singles? If there is information for couples, but little or none for singles, think about how you can suggest this be balanced out.

Announcements in the church bulletin also are a consideration. For example, if your church offers seminars to couples, and singles are welcome, ask that that be stated. Don't assume other singles will know this. Even if they suspect it, they will feel awkward attending unless it is clear to the entire church that they are welcome. When the marriage and family pastor of our church made this evident regarding his marriage seminars, many singles thanked him, stating that they wanted to attend, but weren't sure if they could or should.

Similarly, if your church offers seminars on singles topics, ask the leader to announce that couples are welcome and to emphasize that we *desire* their presence. The leader must help them recognize the value in attending because it's not intuitively obvious. The reason for crossover in these two arenas is different. You may want to attend a marriage seminar either to prepare for marriage or learn more about relating in general. A corresponding pull for couples to singles seminars doesn't exist. Consequently, it is good to communicate in an announcement why it is advantageous for couples to attend a singles seminar. Otherwise they are left wondering why they are invited. Couples who have attended the singles seminars I've given have told me they really benefited by attending.

If pastors and other high-level leaders are involved in or at least periodically attend special single's functions and teachings, this conveys great value to us. For example, all the pastors at my church are highly involved in our single parents' fair. Their visibility communicates that this is an important function and the church strongly supports it. When pastors give a special teaching for singles, this also conveys value. And because pastors are trained in theology and how to teach God's Word, their involvement often affords better quality teaching. Because some of the issues we face pose deep theological questions, this specialized training is much needed at times.

Such involvement by pastors counters an unspoken message that we "hear" when pastors don't attend any singles functions, yet attend or involve themselves with most other types of church events. Their lack of involvement leaves some feeling overlooked, uncared for or that they are worthy of only the leftovers.

Until now, married pastors likely didn't feel they had a place in singles ministry, especially because of the separation factor that the traditional model has tended to foster. But if a church adopts the paradigm shift I've been describing, it should become obvious that married pastors would be a welcome support in meeting the needs of singles.

SINGLES IN LEADERSHIP

A necessary component essential to shifting the balance is to prepare and place more singles into leadership positions. This is "putting your money where your mouth is." If your church's leaders truly believe singles are capable of leadership...if they truly believe we can be good role models...if they truly believe leadership is not a function of one's marital status but a function of one's calling and character...then they must raise up those singles whom God has called into positions of leadership. And there must be no ceiling as to how high we may go. There is no more emphatic way for the church to underscore what it believes about singles than to entrust us with leadership positions. To do otherwise is as good as saying, "You are not capable or trustworthy." No matter how unintentional, this is the message the church has been sending by not raising up more singles into leadership.

Why aren't there more single leaders? Is it because so few today are capable of leadership, or because we have not been properly trained, or both, or something else? Answering these questions feels a bit like answering which came first, the chicken or the egg. One flows from the other. Obviously, some singles simply are not called to leadership. Some refuse to obey the call. But of those who are called and willing, I think there are some who are not capable only because they have not been trained. Some have not been trained simply because their leadership gift has not been discerned. Sadly, however, I think some have not been trained because they've automatically been overlooked simply because they were single. The oversight may be totally unconscious, even on the part of singles themselves. You may have unconsciously disqualified yourself because you've generally not seen singles in leadership. This is why I use the chicken and the egg analogy. For some singles, they are not capable because they are not trained because they are overlooked because they are single. And the cycle continues, so few of us ever enter the starting blocks.

A similar but slightly different factor also fosters this cycle. What we believe about people is often what we'll elicit from them. If we believe a person to be of strong character, that's what we'll draw out. Conversely, if we think little of a person, we will not draw the best out of him or her. Accordingly, there is a correlation between giving people responsibility and the degree to which they will rise to the occasion. If you can trust people with a degree of responsibility, and you give it to them, you elicit the best from them by this demonstration of your trust. You also give them a base upon which to prove themselves and thereby build an increasing capacity for more responsibility.

This is a cycle that calls people upward. (Read the parable of the talents in Matthew 25:14–30.) Taken together, these truths help us understand that the current lack of single leadership tends to convey that the church is *not expecting* leadership from us. It's not eliciting it—not pulling the best out of us. It's possible that where there is an actual (as opposed to perceived) lack of commitment by some singles, it may be because no one is calling them higher. If no one is actively demonstrating a belief in your capability to lead, it is that much harder for you to assert yourself.

Compounding the issue is the fact that those who could assert themselves—those who feel confident in their abilities—may not do so if they feel it is inappropriate to *seek out* a leadership role. Some people believe that they must be approached by a current leader or they'll be perceived as presumptuous or haughty about their abilities. If existing leaders are not pulling the best out of the singles sitting on the sidelines, and the singles sitting on the sidelines remain there only because they are waiting to be recognized, we get stuck in another unfortunate cycle. Potential talent remains dormant.

No matter why there are not more singles in positions of leadership, we have to overcome those reasons. If it is because your church has not adequately trained singles, ask for training. If it is because existing married leaders naturally gravitate toward other married persons to groom for leadership, let's break that cycle by bridging the gap. Whatever the cause, let's get to the root of it and do our part to make the necessary changes.

But let's not buy into the notion that singles are generally less motivated, less committed or less mature. Don't believe that about yourself or other singles you know! It is foolish to think half the population is less capable of leadership merely because they are single. If we could make assumptions across the board that the reason people are single is directly tied to how mature they are or how motivated or capable, then, yes, perhaps we could make such a correlation between capacity for leadership and marital status. But these generalizations about causes for singleness are far too simplistic.

Actually, quite the opposite is sometimes true regarding the "cause" for being single. Some are still single because they have made the very difficult decision, despite their deep desire for marriage, to say *no* to a marriage that would not be right. This takes character. Some have demonstrated great wisdom in knowing when to say *no* instead of *yes*. While some people decided to marry more out of a fear of being alone, some singles decided to instead trust God with their loneliness. Some, in having their desires continually delayed, have demonstrated the type of faithfulness described in Habakkuk 3:17–18:

> Though the fig tree should not blossom,
> And there be no fruit on the vines,
> Though the yield of the olive should fail,
> And the fields produce no food,
> Though the flock should be cut off from the fold,
> And there be no cattle in the stalls,
> Yet I will exult in the LORD,
> I will rejoice in the God of my salvation.

Some, when betrayed by an ex-spouse, have fought the good fight to keep their hearts tender toward God and soft toward others despite their mistreatment. Much can be said about the character, endurance and capabilities of singles. Generalizations characterizing us as uncommitted, unstable or immature are naïve and simplistic.[1] You who have demonstrated the kind of character I just described are some of the best people a pastor could ever hope to have on his or her team!

It is extremely unfortunate that the character exhibited by many singles is not better understood. We attain an incredible depth of understanding into many difficult issues precisely because God uses being single as a crucible for maturation. But our wealth and storehouse are often untapped. It is as if the church is sitting on top of a gold mine with no understanding of the value of the property!

We can relate to many common life experiences and are prepared to minister out of our personal experience. For example, some of us relate to those who experience chronic pain because we have lived with the pain produced when our companionship needs are not met—perhaps for a very long time. Many of us understand challenges that minority groups face because we know what it feels like to be judged merely on the basis of our marital status. You may relate to the disillusioned married person whose life has not gone as expected if you feel that your life did not turn out as expected. In short, a wide range of serious life experiences may be rolled up into the life of *one* single. You can lead others to victory as you have experienced it. You can fulfill 2 Corinthians 1:3–7 by comforting others with the same comfort you have received. What a depth of wisdom and knowledge God has imparted to many of us. Yet, it goes unnoticed.

Frequently, people have responded to me with surprise that I understood their struggles so well. I may say, "Well, I've been single for the last twenty-five years," but it doesn't register with them. They don't understand how that equates to my intrinsic understanding of their pain. Conversely, when a couple, for example, loses a child, we automatically assume that because of what they have experienced they understand a gamut of very difficult issues, especially from the Christian perspective. But generally, this is not so with respect to singles. Our challenges and pain are not understood well enough for people to know the depth of our experiences and how they equip us to minister to others.

One evening I was having dinner with five married women, and much of the conversation concerned struggles these women were having in their relationships with their husbands. After a time, I interjected my thoughts and suggestions on the issues being discussed. All the women agreed with what I shared and actually were quite enthusiastic about the suggestions I made. Then one of them remarked, "Gosh, it's hard to believe you understand these things so well. It's like you were married!" Yes, I *do* understand a lot about relationships. I have worked very hard at having good relationships all my life. You don't have to be married to know how to relate well with people, of the same or opposite sex.

Another time I was sharing a meal with a mix of married and single women. One woman (married) was relating the sad news of a friend's recent divorce. She commented that one of the spouses did not have a lot of moral support on which to rely. The primary reason she gave for this lack of support was that the spouse's best friend was single. "...and so what did *that* friend know?" she asked.

I sat there thinking, *A lot... that single friend knows a lot and could comfort and support that divorcée a lot!* I'll bet that single friend supplied an abundance of understanding about what it feels like to be rejected and misunderstood, what it feels like when your dreams fade into the woodwork and how to press into God when your longing for companionship seems to be more than you can bear.

For these reasons and many more, by all means, let's be sure to advocate broadening the scope of ministry callings for singles. Let's not limit ourselves to singles ministry! Let's not limit ourselves to youth or young adult ministry, which currently is a more common area of leadership for younger singles. Let's help launch other singles in whatever direction God wants to use them!

We do, however, need gifted leaders, married and single, to address singles issues. Various issues must be carefully considered when evaluating a leadership choice for ministry to singles. Should the leader be single? Married? A lot of variables go into this; too many to cover here. But I'll touch on two important points.

First, if a married leader wasn't single for a lengthy period of time prior to marriage, will he or she truly be able to minister properly to singles? Some can. A married person can be a great asset in ministering to singles. And since we are trying to bridge the gap between singles and couples, having a married person lead can be a tangible way to model that. So I don't think you can say a single should always lead ministry to singles.

Second, when a pastor places a leader in charge of ministry to singles, it is important that the pastor assess the potential message the leadership choice sends to singles. For example, if the pastor puts a married person in charge, is the pastor inadvertently sending a message to singles that they are considered incapable of leading? Some people have asked, "Why else would the pastor put a married person in leadership over *singles*?" Consequently, help your pastor understand that if he or she does put a married person in charge, it is best if he or she indicates his or her sincere belief of God's calling on the married person and any other reasons the leader is particularly well suited to minister to singles. It's also a good idea to straightforwardly reaffirm that the church believes singles can be capable leaders. This quells thoughts to the contrary.

I think it's ideal when one or two singles and a married couple lead together. Another great approach for churches that have a marriage and family ministry is to put both ministries under the same umbrella and have the people who lead each ministry work in concert. Both of these options model the bridge, ensure the single-experience factor and send a message that singles are trusted in leadership.

If a pastor truly believes there are no singles in his or her congregation capable of leading, he or she should address that as a *problem*. The pastor should work on grooming singles for leadership instead of merely continuing to place married people in charge. If there truly is no single in your church who could lead, ask God to bring people to your church or to lead your pastor to them. They are out there!

Whether singles are leading in the area of singles ministry or in some other area, the fact that they are serving as leaders can effect major change in your church. By placing them in leadership, your church sends a positive message about singles and upholds role models for single leadership. Your church demonstrates tangibly that there are other valid ways to serve God in addition to being married and raising a family.

Raising up more singles into leadership also naturally opens the door for married leaders to rub shoulders with single leaders. In so doing, married leaders will gain insights into singles firsthand just by having more direct exposure to our lifestyle and needs. This enhances the whole cycle in terms of married leaders better understanding us and thereby ministering to us more effectively and becoming more sensitive to us naturally. Also, the extra exposure single leaders gain to married leaders better equips them for the day they too may marry. It gives them practical glimpses into how to "do" marriage and "do" leadership simultaneously. It's not easy both to lead in the church and maintain a healthy marriage. The more insight a single leader can get about this beforehand, the better.

There also is the "trickle down" effect. Single leaders can help couples in the church at large to understand singles better because of the exposure they give to that lifestyle. It is yet another avenue by which couples gain a realistic glimpse into the life of a single. This helps dispel false images and break down negative stereotypes.

These types of changes need to be made not only on the local level but also on the national level. Because neither singles nor couples are sufficiently reached by national singles ministries, God has another way to fill this void. I envision great single leaders being invited to come alongside married leaders and do national conferences *together*. If done at the national level, it would serve the same purposes and produce the same good results nationally as it produces at the local level.

For example, at PromiseKeepers, single men could join married men in teaching and preaching. They could more effectively reach the *whole* body of Christ by periodically devoting entire messages specifically to singles issues or by peppering messages with more references relevant to singles. Wouldn't that be awesome? Think of the additional men who could be reached by PromiseKeepers if it were more apparent to single men that their unique set of needs would be considered alongside those of married men!

Women of Faith has a gifted single leader in Luci Swindoll and also periodically Kathy Troccoli. They are role models, and united with the married women of that awesome ministry, they all can have a greater impact on their audiences in the same manner. The results could be glorious! By these simple additions, these and other nationwide ministries would reach the whole church more effectively—and almost *half* the church (singles) in a new and freshly relevant way! This is my hope and prayer.

I also hope that the leaders of national family ministries will find it desirable to incorporate into their teachings messages to inspire couples toward friendships with singles. Hopefully they will see the value in integrating singles with families in a healthy, balanced way, and thus promote the development of such bonds by those who follow their ministry.

Conclusion

Tying It All Together

So where does all this lead you if you tie it all together? As you apply solutions from Part I and break free from bondages you may not have even realized you were under, you will increasingly feel better about yourself and about your life. If your relationship with God has been damaged, you'll be able to enter into a healing time. You'll also be well equipped to begin helping others realize the skewed nature of some of the concepts held about and offered to singles. God can use you to open eyes, minds and hearts. The truth sets us free. This is what God wants! He paid the highest price so we could be free. Let's walk in the freedom He so generously offers.

Additionally, as you comprehend, adopt and value the principles outlined in Part II, you'll endeavor to strengthen existing relationships you may have with those who are married. You'll also be willing to take new risks to start building additional bridges with more couples and whole families. You won't feel limited to associating and socializing just with other singles. Your life will be fuller. You'll feel more a part of the mainstream. You'll begin shedding old mind-sets that need not hinder you any longer from enjoying so many of the normal things families enjoy.

As your relational needs are sufficiently met, you'll feel new life being breathed into you. You will gain a sense of belonging to the community around you. You'll give tangible support to others from your overflow. And the more you and others do, the more the church will become a family that welcomes and highly values singles.

As you are making these critical changes personally, remember that others are also. God is changing us not only personally, but corporately as a church. As He continues this

process, bit by bit, your church is going to change for the better. You'll feel it. You'll see it. You'll be a part of it—even an
example for others to follow—to bring about change and
enjoy the fruit of it!

As this insight and understanding spreads, you'll feel seen,
heard and understood when you're at church, working on a
church project or at your home group. You'll feel the strength
of being part of a unit. You'll hear your pastor make references
to things you experience. You'll feel included in churchwide
events. You'll feel respected for who you are as a person without regard to whether you're with or without a spouse and
children. You can hold your head high once again.

The challenges you face and the ones you've overcome will
be recognized. You won't feel alone in them. You'll be validated in your struggles. You'll be given more tools to triumph
over difficulties. More people will come alongside you to help.
And you will believe you have valuable assistance you can give
others, too.

God has placed treasures inside you. You are a storehouse
of His glory. You are not defined by your singleness. He wants
you to shine brighter and brighter with His love, confidence
and joy. Dare to be contagious. Dare to trust God for BIG
things. Push aside the hindrances, and press into being a part
of the family in a way that reflects who your Father is. Enter
into the abundance of joy that is yours for the asking. It is possible. It is attainable. Believe it. Receive it. God bless you as
you run with the vision.

> Forgetting what lies behind, and reaching forward to
> what lies ahead, I press on toward the goal for the
> prize of the upward call of God in Christ Jesus.
> —PHILIPPIANS 3:13–14

Notes

Introduction

1. Jason Fields and Lynne M. Casper, "America's Families and Living Arrangements: March 2000," *Current Population Reports*, P20-537 (Washington, DC: United States Census Bureau, June 2001), 11.

2. Ibid.

Chapter 1: Perspectives

1. Fields and Casper, "America's Families and Living Arrangements: March 2000," 11.

2. Ibid.

3. Ibid.

4. Norval Glenn, David Popenpoe, Jean Bethke Elshtain and David Blankenhorn, eds., "Values, Attitudes, and the State of American Marriage," in *Promises to Keep: Decline and Renewal of Marriage in America* (Lanham, MD: Rowman and Littlefield, 1996), 28; quoted in Linda Waite and Maggie Gallagher, *The Case for Marriage* (New York: Doubleday, 2000), 3.

5. Rose Kreider and Jason Fields, "Number, Timing, and Duration of Marriages and Divorces: Fall 1996," *Current Population Reports*, P70-80 (Washington, DC: United States Census Bureau, February 2002), 16, 19.

Chapter 2: Theological Issues

1. C. S. Lewis, *The Problem of Pain* (New York: HarperCollins Publishers, 2001 edition; copyright restored in 1996; originally published by Macmillan, 1944), 16.

2. Nicky Gumbel, *Searching Issues* (Colorado Springs, CO: Cook Ministry Resources, 1996), 9–25.

3. Several good books have been written on the issue of suffering. I recommend the following: James Dobson, *When God Doesn't Make Sense* (Wheaton, IL: Tyndale House, 1997); Joni Eareckson Tada and Steven Estes, *When God Weeps* (Grand Rapids, MI: Zondervan Publishers, 2000); Philip Yancey, *Disappointment With God* (Grand Rapids, MI: Zondervan

227

Publishers, 1997); Philip Yancey, *Where Is God When It Hurts?* (Grand Rapids, MI: Zondervan Publishers, 2001).

4. Henry Cloud and John Townsend, *12 Christian Beliefs That Can Drive You Crazy* (Grand Rapids, MI: Zondervan Publishers, 1995).

5. One of the many sources regarding the need to consider culture is found in R. C. Sproul, *Knowing Scripture* (Downers Grove, IL: InterVarsity Press, 1977), 101–112.

6. Kreider and Fields, "Number, Timing, and Duration of Marriages and Divorces: 1996," 16, 19.

7. George Barna, "Family," research archive on www.barna.org, visited on October 9, 2002.

8. See also William J. Doherty et al., *Why Marriage Matters: Twenty-one Conclusions From the Social Sciences* (New York: Center of the American Experiment, Coalition of Marriage, Family and Couples Education, 2002); Glenn T. Stanton and Glenn A. Stanton, *Why Marriage Matters: Reasons to Believe in Marriage in a Postmodern Society* (Colorado Springs, CO: Pinon Press, 1997).

Chapter 5: Walking in the Freedom of Truth

1. Douglas L. Fagerstrom, editor, *Baker Handbook of Single Adult Ministry* (Grand Rapids, MI: Baker Books, 1997)), 21.

2. Waite and Gallagher, *Case for Marriage*, 26–30.

Chapter 8: Realities Concerning Loss and What We Lack Relationally

1. *Everyone's* future is "uncertain," but couples tend to have more fixed goals, especially those with children (education, etc.), whereas singles are much more uncertain as to what their future may hold depending on whether they marry, who they marry and where they might live, whether they will have children, etc.

Chapter 11: It's Not Good for Man (or Woman) to Be Alone

1. The Targum for this verse includes, "*I will trample down the walls.*" This is significant in light of the content of chapters 6 and 7, in which we discuss the need to tear down the walls of division between singles and families. Sourced from biblegateway.com as a footnote to the New King James Version of the Bible.

2. Henry Cloud and John Townsend, *Boundaries* (Grand Rapids, MI: Zondervan Publishers, 1992), 86–87.

Chapter 12: Separation for Separation's Sake

1. Some pastors don't know the percentage of singles in their congregation. Consequently, they may assume an attendance rate is good when in reality it is poor.

Chapter 13: Bridging the Great Divide

1. Fields and Casper, "America's Families and Living Arrangements: March 2000," 3; and Tavia Simmons and Grace O'Neill, "Households and Families," *Census 2000 Brief Report* C2KBR/01–8 (Washington, DC: September 2001), 6.

2. When this group was first formed, there was a great need for a small group that would focus on mentoring young married couples, so this group was a tremendous blessing to many couples. But as years passed, people lost sight of the original reason for making it exclusive, and the status quo continued without anything to provoke additional evaluation as to whether the group should continuing being exclusive or return to its original mission with a new group of young couples.

3. This is depicted in many current articles or other publications regarding singles in the church. In addition to Julia Duin's "Why Singles Boycott Churches," see also Rich Hurst, "Building a 'Call-Driven' Singles Ministry," *Enrichment Journal Online*, www.enrichmentjournal.ag.org, visited August 24, 2002; and George Barna, "Church Attendance Drops Again: Boomers Cut Church From Schedule," February 28, 1996, viewed on www.barna.org on June 25, 2002; and Lauren F.

Winner, "Solitary Refinement," *Christianity Today*, June 11, 2002, 30–36.

4. Julia Duin, "Why Singles Boycott Churches," *BreakPoint Online* (January 7, 2002): viewed on www.breakpoint.org, visited June 8, 2002.

Chapter 14: Bridge Building 101

1. Cloud and Townsend, *Boundaries*. See also their other books, including *Boundaries in Marriage* and *Boundaries in Dating*.

Chapter 16: *Friends* From the Christian Angle

1. Historical Census of Housing Tables; Living Alone, U.S. Census Bureau (Washington, DC: 2001), 1.

2. Fields and Casper, "America's Families and Living Arrangements: March 2000," 4.

3. Cindy Humphrey, written in personal newsletter, Spring 2001.

Chapter 17: Tipped Scales

1. *Christianity Today*, June 11, 2001.

2. Viewed on www.wels.net hosted by Wisconsin Evangelical Lutheran Synod, Milwaukee, Wisconsin, visited on June 27, 2002.

3. Dana Anders, Nathan Clement, Chris Conti and Lana Trent, *Single and Content* (Nashville, TN: Word Publishing, 1999), quoted in Lauren F. Winner, "Solitary Refinement," *Christianity Today* (June 11, 2001): 32.

4. Duin, "Why Single Boycott Churches."

5. Mark Chalemin, "Singled Out in Church," *Encourager*, Vol. 9, No. 2 (February 2002).

6. Richard H. Gentzler Jr., "When Recruiting, Don't Forget Singles," *Interpreter* (February/March 2000): published by United Methodist Communications, as viewed on www.gbod.org, visited August 24, 2002.

7. Viewed on www.wels.net hosted by Wisconsin Evangelical Lutheran Synod, Milwaukee, Wisconsin, visited on June 27, 2002.

8. Duin, "Why Singles Boycott Churches."

9. Fields and Casper, "America's Families and Living Arrangements: March 2000," 11; "Marital Status of the Population 15 Years Old and Over, by Sex and Race: 1950 to Present," (Washington, DC: U.S. Census Bureau, 2001), Internet release date, June 29, 2001.

10. Mark Chalemin, "Singled Out in Church."

11. These searches were conducted on July 2, 2002.

12. Although PromiseKeepers is mainly thought of specifically as a ministry to men, a primary focus of PromiseKeepers is strengthening the family, as evidenced by promise number four, which is "A Promise Keeper is committed to building strong marriages and families through love, protection and biblical values." Viewed on www.promiskeepers.org, visited on August 24, 2002.

13. Alan Hedblad, editor *Encyclopedia of Associations*, 39th Ed. (Detroit, MI: Gale Group, 2003), 1297.

14. Ibid.

15. *Family Life Today* website, www.FamilyLife.com, visited on August 24, 2002.

16. Hedblad, *Encyclopedia of Associations*, 2061.

17. Ibid., 1284.

18. *Christian Parenting Today*, *Marriage Partnership*, *Catholic Parent* and *Faith and Family* are nationally promoted magazines for couples. This is compared with *Living Solo* and *Christian Single* for singles.

19. George Barna, "Family," research archive viewed on www.barna.org, visited October 9, 2002.

20. Mark Chalemin, "Singled Out in Church."

Chapter 19: Adding More Weight
to the Other Side

1. I do not provide quotes that I might not dishonor those saying
   such things. Those who make these assumptions don't seem to
   realize one of the things I'm trying to help us understand. If singles feel uncomfortable or out of place in church, *this* may well
   be the reason their commitment and maturity sometimes *seem*
   less consistent than that of couples. Singles who continue to
   serve despite this unfortunate portrayal demonstrate great character, disproving the allegations.

You may obtain more information about
Virginia McInerney by visiting
www.VirginiaMcInerney.com
or writing to:
VirginiaMcInerney@ameritech.net